THE MASTER
AND HIS MEN

J Stuart Holden

THE MASTER AND HIS MEN

J Stuart Holden

AMBASSADOR

BELFAST, NORTHERN IRELAND
GREENVILLE, USA

THE MASTER AND HIS MEN
© Copyright 2002 Ambassador Productions Ltd.

ISBN 1 84030 131 7

Ambassador Publications
a division of
Ambassador Productions Ltd.
Providence House
Ardenlee Street,
Belfast,
BT6 8QJ
Northern Ireland
www.ambassador-productions.com

Emerald House
427 Wade Hampton Blvd.
Greenville
SC 29609, USA
www.emeraldhouse.com

CONTENTS

FOREWORD

THESE addresses are taken from the sermon notes of the late Dr. Stuart Holden. They were delivered by him under the title "The Master and His Men". They were prepared for the Press by his devoted friend, the late Mr. Fred Mitchell, who was also Home Director in Great Britain of the China Inland Mission, as Dr. Holden had been.

How greatly both men are missed. Both had a genius for friendship and for Biblical exposition. The messages of both were much appreciated at the Keswick Convention of which both were Chairmen for a time.

I shall always count it a happy privilege that through our friendship for Dr. Stuart Holden I came to know and love Mr. Fred Mitchell. We enjoyed together going through the beautifully written sermon notes of Stuart Holden which were given to me. There could not be a more appropriate theme for another volume of Dr. Holden's sermons. He loved to talk of the Master and His power over His men, and many became Christ's men through his ministry. He had a great understanding of the human heart through his genius for friendship and no one could know him long without knowing His Master better. Like many other Cambridge men I quickly came under the spell of his ministry, and his friendship has always been one of my most prized possessions.

HOWARD SYDNEY

I

HOW HE CHOSE
AND COMMISSIONED THEM

"And he ordained twelve, that they should be with him, and that he might send them forth to preach" (Mark iii. 14).

A STUDY of history is the best corrective for pessimism. In days when things are none too bright, especially in and concerning the Christian Church; when doleful conclusions and counsels are readily received and expressed by all kinds of people, and we are in danger of indulging in misgivings about the future (which is, did we but know it, just a giving place to the devil!); when we consider arming to defend ourselves, instead of pressing forward to the attack—what we really need to do is to acquaint ourselves with our own history. To study our past, to consider all the way by which the Lord our God has led His people from the beginning, to learn again how well-founded are His plans, to lay to heart the victories by which the cause of the Christian Church is marked, is to remember that God is not dead, that the Ancient of Days is not enfeebled by age, that not one iota of "all power in Heaven and on earth" has slipped or been wrenched from the Hands that once were scarred and now are sovereign. "I will do better things for you than at your beginnings" is the Divine promise which transcends even so lofty a flight of faith.

With the object of reinforcing our Christian confidence and hope with records that are beyond all gainsaying, we shall study the beginnings of the Christian movement by considering the men chosen to be its earliest officers, the central figure in the group being the Master Himself, from whom each derived his competence. It is a story without parallel, full of heartening incentive and challenge. For now, as then, He needs men. The Master still works wonders with poor material and still fashions, out of very ordinary clay, "vessels unto honour" meet for His use, confounding the mighty with the weak. In this study our own ancestors call us to give Him His chance in our day as they did in theirs.

This present chapter is introductory, and its lessons general. Those that follow are intensive and particular.

Mark iii. 14 is one of the "crisis hours" of history. The dividing-line of Christ's ministry had been reached. Up to this time He has been single-handed. Now he feels the need of sympathetic fellowship and a supplementary force. He wants men to whom He can impart Himself in close intercourse, and upon whom He can rely for the extension of the Kingdom He is establishing. So, from among the larger number of those who were beginning to attach themselves to Him as interested hearers, He chose Twelve, inviting them to give up their present manner of life and to adopt His. By this time they knew enough of what His aims were to be aware of some, at least, of the implications of their acceptance.

It is significant that He chose Twelve—corresponding to the number of the Tribes. This, to the Jews, could not but point to His Messianic claim, and identify His works and His words with the fulfilment of the ancient prophecies. With what awe the Twelve must have heard their names called! He did it all with the minimum of organisation. He enjoined no rules, but staked the entire future of His cause upon them, that is upon men who had been "with him" long enough to become themselves captured by His spirit and so to be competent to "go forth" to reproduce Him in the world. "Truth through personality" was His aim.

Each of them was chosen, not from the so-called influential classes, but from the humbler walks of life. They were fishermen, publicans, small tradesmen, unspoiled by the artificiality which was commonly found on the higher social levels of life—simple, unaffected, elemental men, ready to be unconventional because for the most part unacquainted with the conventions. Not that the Master excluded any class; He has no class-consciousness. Nor has He any issue with culture, worldly position, or wealth which is properly obtained, except that those who have these are less ready to become "as little children", to begin life all over again, or to take direction about things they imagine they know already. No, obviously He calls these men because they are just the best He can get, willing to be shaped for use. It is evident that He has other criteria of value in men than those generally employed. Think of anyone starting a movement today, especially a movement with a world-wide objective. The first thing necessary is a list of names, and the more exalted the names the better. Statesmen, financiers, a High Priest or two, Society leaders, novelists, musical comedy actresses, or a film star!—anyone, in fact, who will lend distinction and draw the crowd.

How unlike everyone else Christ is! At every point He could say: "My kingdom is not of this world." Never is this so self-evident as at its beginnings, in His choice of associates. We sing of "the glorious company of the Apostles", but they were just ordinary men who became glorious by being in His glorious company. They were willing to become identified with Him, even though that meant leaving their all. "Not much to leave," you say? Well, every man's "all", however little, is a lot to him; his attitude towards it, when Christ's invitation reaches him, registers his fitness to become one of the Master's men.

These men, of marked contrast to one another in temperament, capacity and record, were somehow welded into a convincing unity by their individual acceptance of the honour of His choice. Their relationship with Him set up a unique relationship with each other. Under one inspiration they actually became "one", a unity that did not attempt uniformity. Each found in Christ the complement of his own need, and the understanding companionship which gave life, and in particular the life of service, its meaning. Each called Christ "Master", and his fellow "Brother". The fact that he was himself appreciated by the Master gave to each an appreciation of the others. Centralised as each was, in Christ, they found themselves conjoined in a bond stronger than life itself. Like stars, each held his place by relationship to the Sun—hence their life together was ordered. It might have been thought that the Master would choose a larger band, having in view so vast an enterprise, but there were enough of them to give Him His chance with almost every type of character, whose virtues and deficiencies inevitably came out before they had been long with Him and each other.

Each of His men brought Him what he had. And the history of the group is simply the story of transforming grace, and of the consecrated use of varied aptitudes in a service in which each supplemented the other. None of them was always complete in his apprehension and loyalty, or always worthy. Some of them were slow learners; and one, at least, broke down under the training and made a disastrous end to a good beginning. None of them avoided disappointing the Master. Some of them, in the strangest way, misunderstood and misrepresented Him. But He never despaired of them, never cast them off, never rescinded His invitation, nor lowered the degree of His confident, open, self-revealing companionship, nor relaxed His grip upon them. We hear of "the perseverance of the saints", but here we see the perseverance of the Saviour, of the Master. And we can appreciate it, for we know that, apart from it, we, like our ancestors, are hopelessly worthless and useless. Yes! He persevered with them, and, in the event, He was justified, for it was by these men that His Word went out into all lands. By these men the tidings and influences of Redemption were carried over continent and ocean. Their names will be found upon the foundation stones of the City "whose Builder and Maker is God". The Master chose His men well.

Consider to what it was He chose and called them: "That they might be with Him" and that "He might send them". To fellowship, and service, not to the one without the other. For fellowship without service tends only to mysticism and even fanaticism, while service without fellowship is sheer presumption, futile mechanism. Together they are as soul and body. It is the tragedy of modern Christianity that they have ever been separated, in an overcare for self resulting in an undercare for the world, and vice-versa.

There is a deeper meaning than that of physical proximity in the words "with Him". It suggests spiritual sympathy, the acquisition of His outlook, aims, and impulses, for which the fact of living and journeying together gave opportunity. These men must become learners before they can teach. They must become convinced themselves before they can be convincing. They must know the reality of the Truth with which they are to be entrusted, of which they are to be the voices. They must become, in recognisable degree, like Him, if they are winsomely to proclaim Him. Their mere declaration of the Gospel—however accurate—apart from personal demonstration, can only be powerless. They must exemplify the potencies of the Evangel; they must adorn the Doctrine. They must commend themselves to every man's conscience, and know how to keep their lives geared on their dynamic resources. They must know how to do always the things that please God, to love when they are unloved, to win by submission, to set the interests of the Kingdom before any other. And this can only be by fellowship with the Master Himself. There is no other way to

Christ-likeness but Christ. "With Him." "For ah! the Master is so fair." Of course this implies a miracle—nothing less, and this is what He covenants. Nothing less! The gift of a new life!

Then "sent forth", gladly and contentedly, actually "put in trust with the Gospel", working out, each one, his own spiritual insights into witness-bearing as unique in character and form as his own fellowship with the Master is unique. These men "came to Him", life began for them, and their story is written for our learning.

There is room for us all—for each of us with our individual history and temperament, with our own peculiarity and capacity, in the fellowship of the King and the service of the Kingdom. And there is only one test of qualification: "Lovest thou Me enough to trust Me?"

II

PHILIP

John i. 43–46.

THERE is no obvious reason why Philip should be the first of the Master's men to be considered, for he was not in the front rank of the Twelve. A significant fact is that neither Matthew, Mark, nor Luke gives him a single mention, beyond recording his name as one of the group called by Christ to be His associates and apostles. His life and record apparently were not such as to make any special impression upon them! They must have known him, directly or indirectly; but there was nothing of outstanding importance about him which, from their individual point of view, called for mention.

John alone, part of whose purpose in his Gospel is to exhibit Christ in contact with various men and women, says anything of Philip. He tells us only three things about him—apart from the incident of his first meeting with Christ and its immediate outcome in the persuasion of Nathanael. But on this very account, that he was an ordinary rather than an outstanding member of the band, the story of his apostleship has an arresting interest for us who are, ourselves, men of ordinary calibre only, and limited range of opportunity. What is told of him, and the plain, unforced deduction to be drawn from it, have a meaning for us which is unmistakable, and an application which is unavoidable. So we consider him first.

He was, in all likelihood, a disciple of John the Baptist; and was the first one to be directly called by Christ to follow Him. Tradition identifies him with the man who said: "Suffer me first to bury my father"—not a plea for the carrying out of an inescapable obligation, but a pretext for delay. If that be so, it helps us see the deliberateness and depth of his choice; and at the same time gives an indication of his character. Under Christ's persuasiveness he gave in. For it is evident that he was a slow-witted man; a man who liked to look well before he leapt—indeed, the kind of man who is disposed to look so long that he is often dissuaded from leaping at all. A dull man, prosaic for the most part, strictly matter-of-fact and unlikely, at any time, to let emotion or ecstasy or feelings of any kind, run away with him. A man incapable himself of anything like exuberance, and impatient of those who might exhibit it. The tiresome kind of man who must "have things down in black and white", as though that makes them any the more trustworthy. But the kind of man who is unlikely to be enticed away once he is committed. All this, and more, comes out in the recorded incidents of his three years with Christ.

It appears, in fact, at the very beginning. On coming into contact with Christ he communicates his discovery to his friend Nathanael, and in terms so precise as to make it clear that already he has become sure of his ground. His respect for the Law and Prophets had to be satisfied; and it is strictly in order when we infer that his first days with Jesus were spent in the Old Testament—with its Living Theme as his Guide. Soon he came to know he was on solid ground, the sort of ground a man must have who knows he has to worship God with all his mind. Philip is the man who not only must know, but must have reasons for his certainty and his hope. By the same token, he can understand and enter into the mental difficulties of others, and when he cannot answer their questions, he knows who can and is not afraid to propose to them the test of experience. He can say "Come and see" because he has seen. Such an one may be unsure about a good many things. He may be spiritually "slow in the uptake", but he always knows whom he has believed —and why; and he is always a helper of the faith of others. Until they come to their own certainty they can always lean on him, and he does not let them down.

Philip comes into the centre of the picture when the hungry crowds on the hillside have either to be fed or dispersed (John vi. 5). It was to him that Jesus put the question, and "this He did to prove him". It was part of the Master's training of His men that they should come to know themselves; and this was the inevitable result in this instance with Philip. His answer was self-revealing. His apprehension of Christ's power was altogether deficient. Fancy talking of two-hundred penny-worth when He is at hand! Here was practicality in the saddle riding him right out of the zone of the miraculous. His temperament got in the way of his faith. He really knew too much arithmetic to be adventurous. Safety first; common sense first; facts first: all these controlling considerations in such an issue revealed the man and must be finally and for ever discredited in his own eyes if he is to be the Master's man in the wide-opening service of the Kingdom. This Christ proceeds to bring about by the miracle—that is, by being Himself. Philip learned something that day about his own wooden unimaginativeness which ought to have been positively recreative. So close doth nature cling to us, however, that it was not. The self in any of us dies hard.

The next mention of Philip is in connection with the request of the Greeks to interview Jesus (John xii. 22). And here it is amazing that he should have answered them as he did, but for the fact that he was the man he was. Again the cautious, ca'canny spirit of the man moves him to discourage these eager seekers. Almost you can hear him: "Not quite sure if it could be arranged." Inwardly he was not quite sure how far it was wise to encourage this sort of thing, foreseeing new complications added to those already existing. It is not difficult to imagine the less self-bound Andrew, to whom he told his misgivings, exclaiming: "Away, man! Don't you know the Master better than that? I thought we had all learnt together on the hillside that to send folk away is the last policy He ever favours. This coming of these Greeks is no calamity. It is the finest encouragement the Master and the Movement has had yet." And it shows what manner of spirit Philip was of that he went along with Andrew and told Jesus. He may be slow, but he's not stubborn; he may be quite awkwardly humdrum in mind, but he is not obstinate. His brilliance may never set the Jordan on fire, but a willingness to be led on will cause the fire to kindle in his own heart ere long. There is great hope for Philip in spite of his limitations. Would that there was the same hope for some of us!

Then in the Upper Room, after the Sacred Pledges had been given and taken and Jesus tells them of the Father's Home and of His Will and His Love, Philip shows himself to be a man of earnest aspiration but dull apprehension, when he breaks in with: "Lord, show us the Father" (John xiv. 8). "The one thing that will satisfy me is some evidence I can see for myself. I find it hard just to walk by faith." What could have been more devastating than the Master's query: "Have I been so long time with you, and yet hast thou not known Me?", or more finally assuring than His complete definition of His ministry, which was to stand Philip—and the entire Christian Church in all ages—in good stead in coming days: "He that hath seen Me hath seen the Father"? The glorious Evangel is that we have to do with a God who is like Christ, not with God and Christ (which idea has given rise to all kinds of confusion—of legalistic theories of strictness placated by sacri-

fice, of angry power overcome by gentle pity), but with
God in Christ.

That is the man the Master "found"; the kind of man
He adjudged as being both suitable for His purpose and
agreeable to His desire for comradeship. Truly He did not
come to find perfection in any one, but to set all who would
in the way of it. And He has a wonderful way—all His
own—of making the best of a man. Just as when the
loaves were given to Him He gave them back, a far bigger
store of bread, so He does with life. We give it to Him
and He gives it back to us, a bigger, fuller, richer life for
its dedication. And whatever may be its ordinariness, or its
idiosyncrasies, or its temperamental limitations, He can
find some value in every life that yields to His solicitations
and is willing to be with Him and to be sent forth. Think
of Philip when you are tempted to self-excusing and self-
depreciation.

So far as we know Philip never achieved greatness, nor
even conspicuous distinction. Endued with "power from
on high" along with the rest at Pentecost, so far as actual
record goes he passes into obscurity (for, of course, he is
not to be confused with Philip the Deacon). Tradition
ascribes evangelistic labours in Northern Syria to him, and
ultimate martyrdom. But the Acts of the Apostles contain
no mention of him; no miracles, no sermons moving multi-
tudes to repentance, no missionary journeys, no epistles to
Churches in whose formation he had taken part, nothing
of that order is associated with his name. The Spirit of
God evidently invested him with power for the heroism
of ordinary, unexciting, even monotonous Christian life
and witness; for membership and probably leadership
in some small church of no renown, carrying out its
ministry of worship and evangelism in the uninspiring
environment of an obscure provincial community. There
Christ used him; there he lived and wrought with such
fidelity as to qualify for one of the Twelve Thrones and to

have his name engraved on one of the City's Foundation Stones.

What would the Christian Church and the Christian cause be without its Philips? These are the men whose experience of Christ is of the plain, simple order, who are not compellingly enthusiastic but who are painstakingly loyal, scrupulously honest, downright sincere. They may not be fast movers, but they are steady, reliable workers; they may not show much eagerness to embrace every new thing before its worth is tested, but their dogged devotion to the old things is to be depended on and marvelled at.

A clear, cautious head doesn't necessarily indicate a cold heart, nor is thoroughness a mark of impiety! On the contrary, it is an evidence of a piety that takes more stock in deeds than in words, in performances than in promises, in duties faithfully carried out than in protestations glibly uttered. Those who have these qualities, and cultivate them in their fellowship with Christ, are beyond value in any church.

Sweet songs are a happy adjunct to Christian life, but steady, undeflected, unwearied purpose is a vital necessity to it. The men who make the really valuable contribution to Christ's service are not the piously pushful, the ready talkers, the perfervid enthusiasts who play at a hundred things and do no one thing with all their might, but those who do justly and love mercy and walk humbly with their God!

It has been well and quaintly said that there are many rooms in the Father's House! It is not all roof-garden whence the landscape and the stars are seen, and where those who are transported by the vision sing their joys. There are ground-floor rooms, kitchens and cellars, where plain men and women do ordinary things for God—without parading the fact; men and women who can be counted on to be on their job whatever the day of the week or the

weather, or the counter-attractions which make appeal to
them to come out and walk some by-path meadow! Philip
was of their number and to such an one as Philip Christ
imparts Himself. Have no fear, then, as to the worth of
your life to Him! All He asks of you is that you company
with Him ; He will send you forth.

III

ANDREW

A S EVIDENCING the fact that the possibilities of Christian fellowship and service are by no means restricted to any one type of natural temperament, and that the Water of Life is contained by vessels of all sizes and forms for communication to a world of variety, a study of Andrew is full of enlightening and encouraging suggestiveness. As with Philip, he comes into prominence on two occasions of outstanding importance to the Master's mission—the feeding of the multitude in the desert, and the visit of the enquiring Greeks. In them, as in the other recorded incidents of his life, Andrew stands out as a great-hearted man, of quick decision and fine courage; a man whose mind was soon made up in an issue, and *stayed* made up; a man to be depended upon for fidelity; a man who brought conscience to the service of conviction. Andrew was the kind of man who, having put his hand to the plough, convinced that ploughing was the right work to engage in and was for him the Master's appointment, never worried as to whether he could do better as a fisherman. No looking back in mental uncertainty ever made his furrow unstraight. Here was not a showy man but an eminently safe man; one whose enthusiasms ran deep rather than wide, noiselessly full rather than babblingly shallow; a man of few words, especially when the hour called for deeds, but one whose words were weighty with sincerity; a man to be studied—and followed as he followed Christ.

A disciple of John the Baptist, it is evident that before his first meeting with Jesus Andrew had been brought under a conviction of sin, national and personal. The flaming preaching of the Prophet had illumined for him the moral messages that had been handed down from generation to generation in the ancient Scriptures, but which had seemed increasingly to lose something of their imperative authority as those who had first voiced them receded into history. He saw, as John's words lit up the foreground of life and the horizon of eternity, that God was alive; that sin against Him was a deadly thing, fraught with terrible consequence to peoples and persons; and that he himself was both implicated in Israel's defection and had an account of his own that must be settled. At once, on realising this, he acted decisively! There was one thing to do and he did it! Consequences didn't bother him! He was the kind of man who saw his duty steadily and saw it whole! He repented of his sin and was baptised!

So far as it was possible and the work of the fishing fleet afforded opportunity, he companied with the Baptist. Whoever else might excuse himself from those daily gatherings on Jordan-side (on the plea that the Temple services were more attractive, or that some of his friends wanted him to go with them to hear a new rabbi who was just then visiting Jerusalem!), you may be sure Andrew never did. He wasn't the man to lose anything that John had to tell about the Coming Messiah. He wanted to learn all he could concerning the Hope and Consolation of Israel. For might He not appear in his lifetime?

And so it happened that Andrew was there on the very day when Jesus came Himself to be baptised, and on the next day also when the Baptist pointed to Him and said—"There He is! Behold the Lamb of God!" At once his decision was made, clear-cut and unequivocal: he followed Jesus. Without any hesitation, he took the step for which his attachment to John had prepared him and up to which it had led him; he changed his allegiance forthwith. While some, even in that day, might be found to charge him with inconstancy, one man, at least, understood and saw in Andrew's attachment to Jesus an evidence of the success of his own mission. That man was the Baptist!

Some people change what they call their "religion" easily. You find them becoming Christian Scientists, New Thought followers, Star of the East gazers, Sacramental Ritualists, without any difficulty. The fact is that in the majority of cases they really had no religion to change. But Andrew had. The God of Christ was not Another from the God of the Baptist, only declared in fuller, clearer revelation. John declared Him in terms of Truth: Christ in terms of Grace and Truth. This was no change of religion, just the decisive action of a man who is made aware of the implications of his religion—a man who brings his life and his allegiance into line with his enlightenment.

Without in any way denying his former experience, pressing on, indeed, to a completer fulfilment of his already pledged loyalty as a man who needs must love the highest when he sees it, Andrew promptly and categorically declared himself. He accepted the Master's invitation and abode with Him where He dwelt that day and night. Where? What did that matter to one who had come to the end of a long quest only to find himself at the beginning of an endless life? What happened that night no one knows, but all may well surmise! The very next day Andrew begins to tell the Good News. He wasted no time trying to be eloquent over it. The News itself is its own convincing eloquence! Good news always is! What could be simpler or ampler than Andrew's "We have found the Christ"?

Of course it takes courage—more courage, unfortunately, than many of us have ever been able to summon—to speak to one's own family, close friends, business associates, in simple terms about the great Discovery. How much easier it is to go out as a foreign missionary than to tell those nearest and dearest to us of the Saviour we have found.

They know us so well, and have the opportunity of watching us so closely. They know if there's any real change in us and can correct our words by our ways. Of all this Andrew was doubtless as fully aware as we are. It is just here that his quality showed itself. He first went after his own brother—and got him! It is likely that he felt (as who does not who comes to know Christ?): "All the world should know this Gospel. Every man ought to have the Truth which sets sinners free." And it is just as likely that he felt: "But it's beyond me. Who am I to evangelise all nations? Yet what I *can* do at least is to win one. And it's up to me to do it. So here goes!" And he made tracks for his brother who, in the providence of God, was to become a far more eminent man in the Master's service than he himself.

I like to think—and the thought develops itself into substantial certainty—that it was not just Andrew's confident confession that he had found Christ that convinced and won Peter to come and see for himself. Nor was it simply the respect he had always held for his upright, steady, dependable, businesslike brother, though that helped, as it always helps. Rather was there something about him, as unmistakable as it was indefinable, that compelled Peter to wonder. A radiance, peace, effluence, had come to Andrew as a result of those few wonderful hours with Jesus. It was not a simpering smile and a shibboleth of the "Hallelujah, brother!" order that never serves any other purpose than that of nauseating healthily-minded people, but an evident inward control, a deepening of personality that pointed to great possibilities, a plain evidence that "sunlight had been added to daylight" for Andrew. It is always that, or something like that, which validates the spoken word and influences others to make their own experiments of faith. There's little use in setting out on the Master's errands without first being "with" the Master in the fellowship that transforms the messenger.

Of course Peter had always been the brilliant member of that family, the one who had always outshone Andrew in everything and always would. In winning him to Christ, Andrew did a bigger thing than he ever knew, until he "stood with Christ in glory looking o'er life's finished story", though by no means had he to wait until then for the reward of his courageous, decisive fidelity.

The same practical promptitude is seen in Andrew's part of the incident in the desert, when Christ fed the hungry crowd that waited until evening, listening to His word. While Philip and the rest were discussing the improbabilities of the situation, Andrew was busy estimating the resources actually available. He it was who discovered the boy with the scanty enough supper in his pocket and set the miracle agoing and the lad wondering as he heard Jesus giving thanks for his supper. The awe and the glory of it all carried the lad out of himself, and his young heart and life were surely there and then given to the Master for keeps, bright gems for His crown. And that boy's soul goes down to Andrew's account, along with his brother Peter's.

Again, Andrew's characteristic decisiveness marked his words and his actions in the situation created by the coming of the Greeks. At once his alert, well-ordered mind grasped the significance of the occasion. At once he brought them —and with them his more hesitant, timid and tentative friend Philip—to Jesus, whom they desired to see. In such an issue as men wanting to have speech with the Master, there's only one thing to be done, and Andrew was the kind of man that does it, and does it at once. The souls of those Greeks, along with that boy's and his brother Peter's, and who knows how many more, go down to Andrew's account. I like to think of Andrew as the model for those whose business it is in the Church to welcome strangers and make them feel at home in the Courts of the Lord's House. A church may be a very unfriendly and lonely place, and will be unless it has some Andrews in its active membership who act as hosts to its guests—the strangers who come within its gates because they would see Jesus. How high is the honour of being "a doorkeeper in the House of the Lord"!

Perhaps the most notable thing about Andrew, however, is his obvious contentment with a second place in the Master's service. He is known, for the most part, in the New Testament as "Simon Peter's brother". He never quite attained to the front rank! Peter, James and John were always ahead of him in their intimacy with Christ and their prominence in the life and work of the group. From the order in which his name occurs in the various lists of the Twelve given in the Gospels, he evidently stood higher in the common estimation than the eight, but not quite with the three. But there is no hint of anything like resentment or jealousy on that account recorded of him; no secretly cherished suggestion that he could do as well as any of them, or even better than any of them—while, as for Peter, well—"where would he have been if it hadn't been for me?" There are no plottings to displace and replace them. Andrew is not even found taking part in the unseemly wrangling of the foremost three as to which should be first, for the man of decision had already decided what was his place: it was to stand by Christ. Beyond this, nothing else mattered to him. Andrew was a self-effacing man, content to fill a little space if God be glorified; an unenvious man who could see a friend preferred before him without inward chagrin and bitterness; who could hear another praised without secret revolt and who could even add his own note to the praise.

Andrew did not belong to the vulgar order of those who can't be happy out of the spotlight, and don't intend to be unhappy. There was simply nothing in common between him and the man who must be first; the man who, if he attends a meeting, must be on the platform if not in the chair; who, if he joins a choir, must sing the solos—or sulk; who is willing to be in the army only if he can be an officer of some rank, and strut; who will play first fiddle in an orchestra, or won't play at all; who just hasn't outgrown the childishness of infant years. Of such are churches blighted! Of such is the Kingdom of God outraged! Andrew is of the order of whose members it is individually written: "Greater is he that ruleth his own spirit than he that taketh a city." His secret was that the Master and His will and His interests and His honour came first— always first with him. With him, decision once made meant decision, and nothing could be of such importance as to rescind it. So he neither envied nor emulated his more famous brother, nor borrowed any reflected light from him. He lived his own life with and for Christ; and it was a full and fruitful life—such a life as we all may live if we love Christ enough.

Tradition credits him with missionary labours in Scythia, and it has always been accepted that he was put to death on the cross with arms of equal length that bears his name, St. Andrew's Cross. Doubtless it is true, for it is impossible to imagine any issue in which this prompt, decisive, courageous, humble man would hesitate in his choice. Death is a mere incident to him for whom Christ, the Lord of life and death, is Master. "How dwelleth, my friend, the faith and love and contentment of Andrew in you?"

IV

PETER

A S IN a garden the same sunshine, showers, dew, nutritive qualities of soil and skilful care of the gardener produce, not uniformity, but variety, both imparting and developing it, so is it in the garden of life; so also in the Kingdom of God. Fellowship with Jesus Christ brings out—transforming them to fine issues——the individual traits of personal temperament, so that, as "one star differeth from another star in glory", the Master's men differ each from the other. Yet each bears convincing evidence of having been with Him.

Strikingly is this so when Peter—in every way the foremost of the group—is considered. For ever in association with the others, he is inevitably in contrast to them all.

His name stands first on each of the lists of the Twelve, which fact in itself is significant. It corresponds with his character as we know it, and with his conduct as we can visualise it from the many available records. He neither understood the cost nor appreciated the necessity of cultivating the background in any situation. He was not the kind of flower that is born to blush unseen! Quick, impulsive, generous, impetuous—he was a man who must express his feelings; a man who, if he sees anything, must say so —must suit his actions to his perception. The logic of facts, once recognised, demanded immediate movement on Peter's part. Adjournments were no part of his make-up. He was "quick on the trigger", a man who does things first and then thinks over them, sometimes sadly, later on. Such a man will make mistakes. But he'll make other things, too, that are not mistakes. Read Matt. xvi. 16.

So frequently is Peter mentioned in the Gospels—and always near the centre of the picture—and so closely is his personal story interwoven with the Great Story, that any-thing like a biographical sketch of him is impossible. Yet his characterisation stands out with quite unmistakable clearness and helpfulness—"helpfulness", for his violent alternations and sheer humanness bring him, at one point or another, very near to us all. For he was, at once, both a very strong and a very weak man.

When called upon by the Master, to whom he had been brought by his brother Andrew, to change his occupation, to give up the lower for the higher form of fishing, he showed no hesitancy. His mind was soon made up, because —unlike some people—he had a mind to make up! It is only too evident that a good many would-be religious people haven't, and take refuge from their own lack of perceptive and decisive judgment in caution, becoming adepts at watching which way the cat is going to jump—a phrase which vulgarly expresses what is going to be the popular or promising thing to do in an issue. Peter is the kind of man who invariably makes the cat jump his way! He left the boat and the trawling gear and the catch forth-with (and with them his visible means of subsistence—and he'd a wife to support, and in all likelihood her mother too!), and attached himself to Jesus.

Of course he had already come to imperative conclusions about the Master. Faith had come by hearing—and seeing. He was taking no leap in the dark but toward the Light! For light had shone in upon Him—searching, scorching light since he'd come into contact with Jesus. Whatever might be in the future it couldn't be darkness since He was in it! So he leapt (if you will!), but he knew quite well in which direction he was leaping.

He saw, with startling clearness, that religion as Jesus

taught and exemplified it was action, not just holding
opinions, nor talking about them in terms of contention.
He'd been sickened to death with that kind of thing by
the Pharisees, who then, as now, loved to indulge in it and
deceived themselves they were doing God service! But it
was doing things, and doing them right now! I love Peter
for many things, and not least because he was so intensely
clear-headed and quick-footed. He was convinced that
religion is a way of living, something to be done, a plan
of life to be carried out—not theorized about, a thing of
the streets and fields and people and the interplay of
human personality. And, being so convinced, he started
in to live and to do it.

When shall we learn that religion isn't a thing to be
argued over by rival schools of thought, but a co-operative
brotherhood of activity? When shall we take in what Peter
so early on learned and proceeded upon, that Jesus actually
meant just what He said (why should we ever think He
didn't?)—that the Kingdom of God is composed, not of
everyone that talketh volubly and, as they fondly believe,
with orthodoxy, about the Will of God, but of those that
get on with it? The blight upon organised religion is the
fostered idea that holding opinions makes a man a Christian, while the plain truth is that the holding of opinions—
however correct—and nothing more, makes a man just the
opposite of a Christian.

When Peter at first came to Jesus, He, knowing him
through and through (just as He knows us all, and as we
know He knows us), knowing his impetuous, unstable, hot,
quick, undisciplined nature, gave him a new name. He
called him "Rock" (Peter), and so gave him something
to live up to! It's not difficult to imagine the quiet
laughs and sly winks of the others when they heard of
it. The idea of Simon being called Rock! It was really
too funny. Was it? Well, the entire story of Peter is
that of a man trying to live up to the Master's expectation

—and promise. For Peter never forgot that this new name (which it is morally certain was to the others, for a time at least, just an amusing nickname!) was given to him in the form of a promise. And he knew the Master meant it—"Thou shalt be Peter"—and would see him through.

Now this impulsiveness, this high-mettled, volcanic eagerness of the man, marked the entire course of his association with the Master.

See him jumping overboard on a dark, stormy lake "to go to Jesus". Here is no waiting to sum up the situation, to consider the improbabilities, to confer with his shipmates as to the wise thing to do under the circumstances, which were novel to them—aye! and to every man under Heaven. His heart ruled his judgment, and he was right to follow it. While mistakes and even follies have resulted from this course—for God has not given men common sense that they should not exercise it—the fact is that far greater follies have been committed, follies running into tragedies, by men allowing their cool minds to override and chill their warm hearts.

See him impetuously rushing in where angels might fear to tread and actually rebuking the Master when it appeared as though the road that led to Calvary might well be abandoned: "Be it far from Thee, Lord!" Just sheer loyalty unrestrained.

See him cutting off the ear of the High Priest's servant in his impetuous effort to defend the Master—while the others looked on, or rather looked round for a way of escape. See him unconsciously revealing himself in his question about forgiving his brother: "Till seven times?" It's a generous, big-hearted man who overleaps injuries and insults and bridges the gulf between the one who has wronged him and himself—seven times over! Here is a man who makes allowances for others because Someone who matters to him tremendously makes allowances for him. There's no cool, calculating consideration here. Just impulsive, quick good nature.

See him—with no illusions about himself—taking no thought of what he was saying and still less of what he was implying, asking the Master to depart from him, to leave him to himself—he's not worth bothering about.

See him, the same impetuous, grown-up child of a man, when the Master actually suggests the possibility of the group leaving Him, taking it upon himself to answer for all of them: "To whom can we go?" If we leave You, we're done!

See him in the Upper Room when the Master is giving them an example that they should follow His steps: "Thou shalt never wash my feet!" And how quickly he took his words back—charmingly inconsistent—when he saw what it was the Master was at: "Not my feet only, but also my hands and my head!"

See him racing to the Tomb, and going right into the grave in search of the lost Master.

See him in the grey morning-light, too impatient for the boat to make the shore on which the Master is seen standing, looking seaward. See him girding on his fisher's coat and wading ashore, possessed by one thought only, that of getting to Jesus at once. A bit too unrestrained and emotional, you say? But what magnificent affection—more convincing to its Living Object than a whole lifetime of sober lukewarmness.

See him later, when the responsibility of his commission is a pressing consciousness, when, having been with the Master, he is 'sent forth' by Him. How unhesitating, even audacious, is the quality of his faith in action!

Go back a bit, and see Peter in what was—quite unknown to him—the great crisis of the Master's cause, and of his own life as one of His men, also. Jesus has just asked the group: "Whom do men say that I am?", and they have "hum'd and ha'd". "Well, there's a difference

of opinion. Some say one thing, some another; some say
Elias, Jeremias, John." "Whom say ye?" and they're
none of them sure enough to say anything. But Peter
blurts out: "Thou art the Christ!" He simply couldn't
have done anything else. His own experience prodded him,
and he didn't need prodding twice. He just could not deny
himself. He knew and therefore he spoke, and didn't
consider his words, either. He had seen the Master's
power too often to be either uncertain or silent. There
was that day when his wife's mother had been healed,
and that night when he himself was drowning! And those
lepers! And that blind man! Most of all there was that
influence that had got hold of him, and was actually
making a new man of him! So, impetuous as ever, he
spoke right out, and there was nothing tentative about
his confession, because there'd been nothing tentative about
his experience.

Of course he had the defects of his qualities. That kind
of man always has. We all have; only with most of us
there's far more defect than quality. Unconsciously he
overrated his strength—"unconsciously", because it is impossible to imagine Peter ever sitting down and analysing
his emotions, feeling his spiritual pulse, taking his spiritual
temperature or blood pressure! That kind of man is never
good for much; for his religion is only a form of self-
centredness, and isn't the religion of Christ at all! Peter
unconsciously began to think of himself as competent. So
he was—for big things, but little things did for him. So
we have the shameful story of his denial of the Master.
It was out before he knew it; before he had time to bite his
tongue out (an hour later he'd have given his all if he'd
only done it!). And, of course, one denial led to another,
and to the quick uprising of the old nature he thought was
dead, to "cursing and swearing"—fisherman's talk, the
strange oaths of the quayside and the fish-market. His old
impetuous, impulsive, hotheaded self had slipped from its

new control and flung him into the bottomless pit of remorse. But that's not the true measure of the man. To know that, see him weeping bitter tears—tears that burnt his eyes like acid. Any man can be overtaken and over-thrown. A little man will excuse himself; comfort himself with a text or two which, under the actual circumstances, he's no right to use. It takes a real man to be genuinely/ sorry, not that he's been found out but that he has failed the Master. There are tears which God puts into His bottle. They're worth preserving! They're the tears of a man like Peter.

Who shall say he didn't learn the lesson of his un-suspected weakness? See him at Pentecost standing up in fanatically Jewish Jerusalem and charging the Jews with the Master's murder! See him before the Supreme Council, having already made acquaintance with the inside of prisons, declaring "we ought to obey God!" Watch him throughout the course of recorded history, and in the self-disclosure of his letters—the letters of a man who im-pulsively poured out all that was in his heart. And what see you? Just a man, never perfect, stumbling—but always in one direction, and always trying to live up to his name and to live out his convictions. Increasingly he realised Christ's saving power, in whom he knew himself "redeemed by His precious Blood"; by whom he was "kept unto salvation" as by the power of God; from whom he received "all things that pertain to life and godliness". Beholding this, we understand what Christ meant when He said: "On this rock I will build My Church"—on a redeemed life, a life that has first-hand experience of regenerating power. For such a life is always a foundation-life. It is Christ-won, and becomes by transformation of natural quality, as well as by impartation of spiritual reality, Christ-like. It never ends with itself!

Such a life was Peter's. Impulsive, impetuous, en-thusiastic to the end, but to the end controlled by that power to which all other power yields, the power of a Love that answers love.

The Master wants men of all kinds—Andrews and Philips and Peters and lesser folk too. He wants you! Don't make the fatal mistake of regarding your temperament as your excuse. It is your equipment.

V

MATTHEW

IT HAS been well said that what God has created and bestowed upon a man at his birth, He does not destroy nor take away from him at his re-birth. A man carries over into the Kingdom of God when, by faith in Jesus Christ and in response to His invitation, he enters it—just himself. Under the refining discipline of the Holy Spirit he inevitably loses many of the unlovely things that have fastened themselves upon his personality; just as he acquires moral qualities which, of himself, he could never acquire. And all that he may become, increasingly, his true self, the man God intended him to be, an unique being, altogether individual and not a weak copy of another. This explains the variety of faith's expression in Christian personality and magnifies "the manifold grace of God". It explains the amazing contrasts to be found in the Master's first group of men. Each one is essentially himself. Each makes his own peculiar contribution to the Cause. In the corporate life of the group each develops his own personality under the inducements and incentives of the Master's companionship. They are not units in an army dressed and drilled to uniformity; they are members of a family beautified by diversity. Each is entirely himself, the more truly so because each is entirely and individually the Master's man—"with Him" in the deepest dependence, the fullest loyalty, the most urgent purpose of his being. And it is to the praise of the glory of His grace that He makes use of this diversity and welds it into a trusty unity for the carrying out of His redemptive purposes in the world.

All things considered, the Master's choice of Matthew is perhaps the most astounding of all His choices. At any rate it was to the people of that day, for by common consent Matthew, although a successful business man, was outside the pale. He was one of a number of Jews whose names were only mentioned in execration. Unpatriotic renegades! Tax-collectors for the Roman conquerors, and tax-farmers of the local rates—for themselves! Men who were conscienceless in exploiting their authority, grinding down the faces of the poor, harassing the rich, flaunting every proper consideration in the ruthless exercise of their detestable office. Rich, of course; and yet how poor, for the best things they couldn't buy. Nothing could exceed the contempt in which they were held. "Publicans and sinners"; "Publicans and harlots"; "A heathen man and a publican" —these were some of the ordinary classifications of Matthew and his chosen associates in the ordinary speech of the time. They were not all bad, only it was a demoralising business which demanded a man's all, and it was a miracle if any man engaged in it escaped demoralisation. Religion was about the last thing anyone would ever think of connecting with a publican. And yet in the end of the day we find Matthew among the Master's men, at the Master's invitation.

Look at him! He was evidently a keen man of business, with the capacities and faculties that go to make up an effective business qualification, and there was nothing to be ashamed of in that. On the contrary, the mental equipment of an efficient man of business is just as much a thing to be proud of and thankful for as the gifts of the artist, the musician, the doctor, the writer. And, as it subsequently proved to be in Matthew's case, it was just as useful in the service of the Kingdom of God. So long as there's nothing devious about it, so long as he's the master of it and it isn't the master of him, a business man has as much right to put a high value on the importance and influence of business as any other men upon their calling.

But that's just where Matthew's case puzzles us—in respect of the Master's choice of him. For the odds were heavily against his business being on the square, against a publican being anything other than a rascal in a privileged position. Matthew evidently had the requisite knowledge and ability to be able to assess the taxes on all the merchandise carried by the caravans along the high road from the seacoast of Tyre and Sidon to Damascus, which ran along the shores of the Sea of Galilee by Capernaum. And having it, he sold it in the best market—which happened to be the Roman market. He was a typical Jew with a characteristic flair for finance, an eye for the main chance. Probably he was a lover of money and determined to make it, little thinking that as its way is—it might unmake him. At any rate, whatever scruples he may have had on the score either of patriotism or religion (and his name "Son of Levi" suggests that he had a religious upbringing and, at one time, actually carried out a Levite's duties in connection with the Temple worship) were overborne by considerations of the profitableness of the Roman Civil Service, and he became a publican. A little thing like religion could not be allowed to interfere with a career, to stand in the way of business. He had to be a Sabbath-breaker, of course; that was a condition of the service. Rome saw to that! But what of it? "Business is business." The race is to the swift, and no man can make success if he allows competing interests to engage his attention. Keen—that's what he must be—keen! And that's what Matthew was! A man to be feared as an official (for he could make things distinctly unpleasant if he chose), and loathed as an individual—a pro-Roman and an apostate Levite to boot. No one of all those who knew him saw anything in him but the detestable qualities of a nest-feathering publican. But "Jesus passed by and saw a man" (Matt. ix. 9). He always does see the man beneath the overlay of his occupations and preoccupations. He always does see the reclaimable man—the man that may be in the man that is! He always does see the man that the man himself doesn't see and can't see.

That is the explanation of the Master's summons—"Follow Me". He saw the man behind the publican, and what He saw moved Him. Was it secret dissatisfaction, and the empty weariness of one who has reached a goal only to find it really wasn't worth reaching, that He saw? Was it the pitiful disillusionment of one who has discovered that in the country of his need the coin of his achievement is not accepted currency; that what he has won't purchase what he wants? Or was it just a fine fellow hiring himself to base uses and fast spoiling himself for the best things that He saw? In all likelihood it was all these and more, for He saw all there was to see! And believing in the possibility of what He saw, He gave Matthew his chance. Quick as light, the business man in him estimated relative values and decided to become one of the Master's men there and then!

Dr. Alexander Whyte makes the ingenious suggestion that Matthew had already long been acquainted with Jesus; that He was often, during His carpenter years, in Matthew's toll-booth paying the taxes levied upon the shop and its takings; or remonstrating with Matthew at the injustice and harshness of his demands which were crushing the life and spirit out of the little trading community at Nazareth, or even going bail for some poor unfortunate who couldn't meet his liabilities. It may have been; who knows? For those are just the things He would do as a good citizen and a good neighbour. It may have been that even then Matthew had been aware of a strange, searching, disquieting, self-accusing influence that seemed to be part of the Carpenter and that made his own "success" look tawdry and shop-soiled. Perhaps Matthew hadn't been altogether surprised when he heard He'd left the bench and the shop to His younger brothers and become a kind of Prophet-Preacher! At any rate it isn't difficult to believe that this was not his first meeting with Jesus. The successful business man in him would hardly have taken the risk involved had he not known something about the One who offered him a partnership in an enterprise which necessitated as qualification the investment of his all.

One can rather imagine him, hearing of the words and deeds which exalted Capernaum to the very heavens (for they were being talked of everywhere—and certainly on the lake-front), and leaving the office to a clerk while he went off time and again to listen and see for himself, wishing—how earnestly—as conscience began to move, that he'd come across Jesus before he'd got his life all tangled up, before he'd been so successful! Going back with a sigh to his ledgers, he realised that the relentless business machine had got him—that he must go on as he'd begun. Then, without warning, the Master appeared and put up to him the most overwhelming proposition of his business career: nothing less than that he should change over from being a publican and become a pilgrim.

What profound courage the Master showed in this! To fly in the face of popular opinion, to flout common prejudice by recruiting a publican, was to ask for trouble. Nothing could be more certain to set people talking not only about Matthew (they'd said all that could be said about him long since) but about Him. Which is just what they did, only to evoke from Him the glorious Evangel that it was just lost men like Matthew He had actually come to save! It says much for Matthew that he could respond there and then, close with Christ's offer and commence forthwith the new life. For it meant that his books were all made up and balanced, that his accounts were in order and his cash balances correct—all ready to hand over. "He rose: left all: and followed Him!" That's the business man who knows that a thing worth doing at all is worth doing now; that delays are dangers; that promptitude is one of the secrets of success! Jesus had set him on the quest for success of a higher value. Of course, there must have been an unrecorded secret interview in which sins were confessed and backslidings deplored and all sorts of adjustments made and promised, and in which Forgiveness and Adoption and Covenant Mercies were declared. Let no man doubt that! And Matthew went on as he had begun. We see him a successful man abandoning his success for a greater. The talents which had made him what he was in the world of business were at once put at the Master's disposal, and He baptised them into service; so that all we ever see of Matthew, in the unfolding of the Gospel story, is of a man trained to accuracy, quickness, keenness, publicity, using all he has—and being used—in the Master's business.

Look, for example, at the means he employed to confess his changed allegiance; and at the same time to bring his old associates and his new Master together! How wise and far-seeing and sound! How immediate! How reminiscent of clinching a bargain so that there could be no going back from it—and he knew himself well enough to distrust himself unless he is committed beyond recall! He did not go the round of the publicans and invite them to a prayer meeting. Mind you, a prayer meeting is a grand thing, and some people would be all the better for making active membership of one a prominently important and regular feature of their lives. As a matter of fact they're suffering from arrested development of Christian personality and are excellent specimens of stunted growth and impaired vitality just because they don't. But Matthew knew his men! A prayer meeting, or even a preaching service, would not have appealed to them in the slightest. He approached them on the side to which they were open—their geniality and good comradeship, their sense of professional fellowship, and he invited them to a meal. He knew that a social gathering of that sort, with the Master present, must mean something great for every guest. In giving them their chance of meeting the Master on that footing, he knew that he would be giving the Master a chance with them! And he knew that He would make the most of it. The making of contacts is one of the first arts of business.

What a crew he got together: "A great company of publicans and others." It isn't difficult to imagine what the "others" were like—"sinners" to a man and to a woman, just the type that would consort with those unscrupulous capitalists. A room full of rich outcasts, up and outs, a sadder sight far—today, as then—than a gathering of poor outcasts, down and outs! There was not a really respectable person among them! And the Master, not patronising the occasion and spreading constraint among these free-speaking guests who knew each other well and called each other by their first names and were well-accustomed to conviviality, but one with them, just Himself!

Little wonder that the orthodox were stirred to fury at such an exhibition of inconsistency! It's curious how the proudly orthodox can work themselves up into a fury at times. How mean and bitter of speech the doctrinally sound can be! Anything like Christian love in action makes them amazingly mad, and causes them the kind of distress that can only be appeased by spiteful and truth-despising criticism and gossip. What a queer product of the religion they profess—which, of course, isn't really religion at all— these Scribes and Pharisees and their succession are! All they can do is to bespatter the Master's Name—"He eateth with publicans and sinners! That shows the kind He is! Just a gluttonous man and a wine-bibber!" Unconsciously they paid Him the richest compliment.

Who told Matthew that Christ's religion was essentially social, a thing to be shared and not to be thought out, or preached out, or even prayed out, but worked out in the social contacts and correspondences of life? It was just the business man's instinct for expansion, for securing new patrons, for making profits—illumined by the Master's Spirit. Later, Matthew's instinct was more than confirmed by the Master Himself who set up as a permanent memorial of His work for men not a pulpit but a Table and a Social Meal. Of the actual results of Matthew's feast we can only conjecture, though at least two publicans—the one Jesus saw praying in the Temple, and Zacchaeus, the chief assessor of Jericho—were probably influenced there for time and eternity. The converted business man was content in the knowledge that he had set forces in motion that could take care of themselves, and that he had, so far as he himself was concerned, hung up his new sign in such a way as to be committed, and so safeguarded for the rest of his life.

Then Matthew brought over into the service of the Master his business man's habit of making a note of things. Indeed it is fairly certain that he had mastered the art of abbreviated writing—the ancient fore-runner of modern stenography—and made use of it to report the Master's sayings. It would almost appear that, as Judas became treasurer, Matthew became secretary of the group and kept the records, for we owe to him nearly all the Sermon on the Mount, obviously not reported from memory! Many other things the Master said which the others missed, especially things that would at once appeal to the keen, active, "cause and effect" mind of Matthew. For example, His safeguarding of deeds as the only valid expression of belief, and of fair-dealing and plain truth-telling and courtesy, as characteristics of the Christian life. His stories of the treasure hid in a field, and the pearl of great price, and the cost at which they are acquired—all a man has! His plain telling of the sheer impossibility of serving two masters, God and Mammon (how well he knew this!); of the foolishness of laying up treasure in insecure places and enterprises; of the eternal question of profit and loss, and the eternal folly of bad bargaining—a soul for the world! Yes— and his verification of events with historical documents "that it might be fulfilled". We begin to wonder what the

Master and the group would have done without Matthew! And what should we have done? For many of us owe, under God, our souls to him and to his testimony to Christ —since it was he who reported the word which opened heaven to us: "Come unto Me" (xi. 28). Thank God for ever for the so-far-successful business man who, coming to know Christ and His power, made it his business henceforth to serve Him in his own way—in a business-like way —and became His biographer. Who could have imagined that such use could ever be made of such a one who modestly refers to himself as "Matthew the publican" that others may be helped by knowing that all the Master's men were not blameless, to begin with, whatever they became, and who passes into obscurity, never to die!

All of which means to us that the Master has need of the so-far-successful business man and woman still. And that, not away from their business, for the most part, but in it. There's a wonderful Gospel waiting to be preached by those who handle ledgers and typewriters and letter-files, cash-registers and adding machines, price-lists and discounts, debits and credits, contracts and acceptances, balance-sheets and stocks and reserves, production and output, sales and maintenance costs, insurances and bills of lading and advertisements—and to be preached in their actual handling of them! For when this is done as unto the Master by those who are first, last, and all the time His men, in His spirit and manner, and as His present commission, they who do it become themselves better men. They send out into life influences as purifying, sweetening, life-giving as the summer sunshine, with consequences too many and too great to be realised by them, but which gladden the Master's heart, helping to bring about the travail of His soul. That's making a success of life! No man does what Matthew did alone. In business there are always those who follow you if you follow the Master— though they may not, at once, follow the whole way.

Apostles are always Epistles, whether they write them or not!

Even though, like Matthew, your life has been so far wasted in the service of "other lords", the Master says "follow". And there is implicit in the invitation the full power and promise of entire restoration to those who will begin now. There are no limits to the reclaimableness of any man, nor to the possibilities of his renewed life, if only Christ is enthroned. He wants to send His saving word to others by you. Will you let Him?

VI

JAMES

THERE is apt to be some confusion about James because there are three of that name whom we meet in the New Testament:

(i) James, the brother of John, the son of Zebedee.

(ii) James, "the less", also one of the group, one of the two "unknown" apostles.

(iii) James, "the Lord's brother", who doesn't figure in the original group at all, but only became one of the Master's men after He had gone; the writer of the Epistle that bears his name.

Apart from that confusion, being clear as to the James in question, though there is not a great deal told of him, there is enough to help us construct a convincing and altogether inspiring record of fellowship with the Master, and a story of service under His direction with the incalculable consequences which always attach to what He does through those who give Him the opportunity of a committed life. Just as from a small arc the mathematician can, without difficulty, describe the complete circle to which it belongs, so from the few details furnished about James anyone whose aim it is to be in the same living contact with the Master as gave significance to his life and career can follow his course and mark its lessons and draw its influences and inferences into his own life for its enrichment and betterment. For here is not the example of a great man that is depressing to lesser men like us who know that life's course is already laid out for us on an infinitely smaller scale than theirs, and that nothing can ever make us be and do what they were and did. Here is the encouraging example of one James, the son of Zebedee, who was himself well within our own range. Not a flaming comet; nor yet a fiery planet; but just an ordinary, steady-shining fixed star, one of the myriads in the Milky Way that together write the story of God's glory across the Heavens.

To begin with he was a fisherman and received the Master's invitation to join the group at the same time as his brother John. The fact that he is always named first ("James and John" not "John and James") suggests that he was the elder of the two, and had to submit to what would have been, to some men, the chagrin of seeing his younger brother become a much more prominent member of the group than himself. But what would have irritated a lesser man to envy does not appear to have affected James in any way. From the beginning to the close of his career he was moved by a quiet devotion to the Master that made every consideration beyond loyalty to Him utterly negligible. He was not interested in what others might do or become so long as he was privileged to make his own contribution to the glorious Cause. "Love one another, and mind your own business" might well have been his motto. It's a grand motto for all Christians; though unfortunately it sets a standard which seems to be too high for many Christians to reach. Not that he was an impersonal, effeminate "lady-like" kind of man—the kind that takes up religion because in no other circle of interest has he the slightest chance of being even noticed, and at the back of whose professions and protestations there lies an impelling egotism, a vast selfishness. As a matter of fact the Master called both the brothers "Sons of Thunder: Boanerges", which is an indication, not of violent, headstrong temper and unrestrained speech, but rather of zeal, enthusiasm, overpowering masterfulness and determination —men who could hold their own and carry their point by the steady weight of their personality. James was by no

means a cipher, a man of no count in ordinary affairs, one
who had no place to lose in the life of the community by
joining the Master. He brought into the life and work of
the Kingdom the appreciable contribution of a definite personality—all his own. And throughout the remaining few
years of the Master's life, and then—past the Cross, the
Resurrection, the Ascension, the Day of Pentecost, into
the life of the Early Church, until he sealed his faith with
his blood, he is seen—the quiet, strong, steady, dependable man, working out his convictions and his indebted-
ness, in consistent devotion to the Master's interests among
men.

It was quite early on that he became one of the inner
circle with Peter and John. And—by the way—it brings
the Master nearer to us to recognise that in this He was
like ourselves: He had intimates, those He quite evidently
cared to have with Him above others; possibly because
He felt there was more in common between them. Certainly
He was not capricious. In all likelihood there was, in the
first instance, just that mutual attraction of personality we
are all acquainted with, which as time went on developed
into an intimacy that conferred both privilege and obligation upon the three. It is perhaps easier to account for
Peter, the natural leader, and John, the ardent mystic, being of that inner circle than it is to account for James. For
unlike either of them he seems to have possessed no striking
characteristics nor any outstanding gifts marking him out
for prominence. He was, by every indication, a silent man,
modest, quiet, retiring, unaggressive, of the order of the
deep-flowing still waters, not of the babbling brook variety,
of which the ranks of religious folk were over-full in Christ's
day as, indeed, they are in this day too.

By every token, the Master appreciated him above
even His ordinary measure of generous appreciation. Christ
even leaned upon him in times of special stress, and used
him, and has been using him ever since. For on three

memorable occasions, in events which were actual crises in the Master's course, He took James with Him! In His first encounter with death at the house of Jairus; in His transfiguration; and in His agony in Gethsemane—He takes James with Him, for support and sympathy and the sheer strength which an understanding friend can minister when spirit is attuned to spirit. We all know what that kind of silent comradeship of discernment can be in hours which seem to crowd lifetimes into themselves! How precious is its balm in hours of sorrow, suffering, high-strung joy! We all know too, the chattering people who spoil the beauty of the music or the wonder of the sunset, if only by insisting on "how lovely it is"; the self-conscious folk who must talk in the presence of sorrow they don't even understand, like Job's friends who were a help to the broken man so long as they were silent in their sympathy —those who haven't an idea that their well-meaning words are like salt in a wound and almost make their recipient scream! Perhaps it was because James was a man who could be silent when silence is golden, and understood because he cared deeply enough, that the Master chose him to be a companion of the high hours and leaned on him as a friend to be depended on.

There are some people who don't say much at any time because they've nothing to say on any subject except themselves! That's the only subject to which they give any thought—and it's never out of their thoughts! Their silence is never an understanding silence, never a thoughtful silence, never a silence of the depths, never a silence of sympathy, and of a look and a hand-grip and a shy caress vibrant with feeling. It's just the silence of selfish stupidity, for self-centredness always is stupid. Let not such people imagine that the Master has any use for them whatever. They're disqualified from the start! But James' characteristic silence was the very opposite of theirs. He just couldn't talk for talking's sake! Words didn't come easily to him, especially when the subject in question went so deep and meant so much as the truth the Master was teaching. The things of the soul were matters to be pondered and prayed about, and diligently practised—to James; not to be peddled and prattled and paraded on every occasion.

It's no mark of reality or of value, for a man to be an overfree talker about the profound sublimities of the Christian Faith. It's easy for some people to talk because it's difficult for them to think—so difficult that they don't do it at all. They simply repeat the tested convictions which others have reached by sore travail, with a light-hearted jauntiness which advertises their meaninglessness to them. And though their words may be "sound" enough —in fact their soundness is one of the things they're proudest of—they're nothing but sound! The only people they impress are themselves! And if you could buy them at their proper valuation and sell them at their own you'd soon be amazingly rich! But they're not in the market! They want themselves so badly that no one else wants them at all. I only mention them as a foil to the quality that made James what he was to the Master and to the cause. He was not one of those who say glibly and far too often for sincerity: "Lord, Lord," without ever having the slightest intention of letting their sentiments rule their lives. He was one who just did the Will of God as he apprehended it from the Master, said nothing about it, and so entered the Kingdom of spiritual fellowship and achievement. In any issue the Master knew He could count upon his loyalty. Happy is the man, and rich in the deepest satisfactions of life, of whom it can be said: "He never let a friend down," and never this Friend, to whom he owes everything! James may not have had Religion at the end of his tongue; but he had it at the tips of his fingers! That counts in religion, for it means something to the Master and to the work He has in hand.

It is certain that James did not elbow his way into the inner circle, nor did he put on airs when he found himself there, as though his humbling privileges were a cachet of his superiority to others. He was one of the order of "the quiet in the land" whose confession is: "Not more than others I deserve but Thou hast given me more." There are some who simply must be to the fore. They've such a large idea of their own ability and importance that they feel the occasion—any occasion will do!—demands it. If no one puts them forward they'll find some way of fending for themselves in the matter. They must get into the lime-light somehow—if necessary by pushing someone else out of it. If they only knew how pitilessly it shows up their blemishes, they'd be less childishly happy than they are. Certainly they'd be less complacent. It never occurs to them that they look ridiculous; any man who is overplaced by his own efforts always does. By the same token, any man who is so looked on by other and more sensible people can never be useful. The lure of office makes a fool of many a smallminded man, to his undoing. But James was not of that sort. No one marvelled more than he did that the Master should choose him. No one of the group more worthily adorned the doctrine, or more completely justified the choice.

He had a frankly impossible mother, one of those women whose foolish fondness spurs them to ambitious efforts for their children or husbands which are their greatest embarrassments. She went to the Master one day, presuming on her kinship to the Virgin Mother, and asked for James and John the chief places in the coming Kingdom. Like so many others she thought Jesus was going to overturn the Romans and set up a Jewish monarchy and that there'd be some fine plums to be picked in the way of high administrative posts. Of course she made James blush—that sort of woman would make an angel blush—by her obtuseness and her mix-up of religious talk and worldly advantage.

Fortunately he'd seen through his mother at an early age, and had cultivated the very opposite quality to her stirring, pushful disposition. When the Master turned the subject—as only a great Gentleman could—by asking the brothers a question that had nothing whatever to do with her vulgar solicitation: "Can ye drink of My cup and share My baptism?"—in other words: "Do you love Me enough to go through this business of the Kingdom of God with Me?"—very quietly and with fine restraint and without a trace of boastfulness they replied: "We can: we do." And the Master left it at that. He and James understood each other. There were no conditions attaching to James' consecration; there were no strings to his commitment.

Once only is anything recorded of this unobtrusive, deep-feeling man which might seem as though he'd misquoted himself (which, of course, is what no man ever actually does when he speaks indeliberately). It is his outburst against the Samaritans who would not receive the Master into their village: "Shall we call down fire from Heaven and devour them?" But there's this to be said for him: his suggestion may not have evinced much love for them, but it voiced a great indignant love for Him. It was a blunder of devotion. It showed that hidden below the quiet placidity of James' steady-going, ordinary, almost speech-less service, there burned hot fires that leaped up in pas-sionate protest at an affront made to his sovereign Lord! Everyone of them burned for Him and for Him only! An insult to himself he might have passed over in silence; for since he'd been companioning with Jesus a great change had come over him. The old fisherman-quickness with oath and blow had been wonderfully controlled. He'd somehow learned to care a great deal less about himself than he used to do. But an outrage upon the Master—that's another matter. He couldn't suffer that in silence. And if he did "spill over", it was the spilling-over of a cup filled to the brim with strong love! Happy is the Master to have such

a friend as James! And thrice-happy is the man who has
it in him to be such a friend! To be a Jonathan to another's
David! To blaze out in defence of his friend's name! To
involve himself, to his own hurt, in his friend's cause,
making it his own! He may blunder over it, as did James,
but he never fails to bless Him whom his soul loveth! I
don't wonder the Master simply had to have James as one
of His constant intimates.

It's hardly surprising that this unspectacular man was
the first one of the group to be martyred for Christ's sake.
Herod was really afraid of the quiet power and influence
of James. So long as he was its leader, the king could do
nothing at all with the infant Church. Neither his gifts nor
his growls, his patronage nor his threats, could curb its
activities nor silence its testimony to Jesus of Nazareth,
whose Name he hated. James didn't declaim, nor do anything theatrical in the way of defiance. He just went on
steadily seeking first the Kingdom of God and His Righteousness when all about him was going the other way. And
the Church was kept true, in its day of testing, largely
because of his quietness and confidence, and a certain
dignity that marked his life. He set a standard for it. That
was James! And it was almost inevitable that Herod
should put him out of the way, though in doing so he made
a tragic mistake for himself. The body of such a man may
moulder in the grave, but his soul goes marching on! And
its march means the downfall of Herod and all like him!
In the end of the day it's the James's who'll sit on the
Thrones!

They don't martyr the Master's men in that way today.
There's no fear of our being killed. It might perhaps be
better for the cause of religion if there were. But sneering
cynicism, rude ridicule, unfeeling contempt, flippant god-
lessness, cultured paganism, the tide of easy-going but
absolute conventionality are just as determined to snub,
silence, and secure themselves against the upsetting in-

vasion of vital religion as ever Herod was. The conditions
of the service are exactly what they've always been: "Let
him deny himself." But

> He who would valiant be
> 'Gainst all disaster
> Let him in constancy
> Follow the Master!

He never lets His men down!

VII

SIMON THE ZEALOT

THERE is one phrase in common use in our worship which more than any other seems itself to be characteristic of the Gospel. We have no hesitation in using it as we do in prayer and intercession, simply because it so entirely expresses the "length and breadth and depth and height of the Love of God" to which it is responsive. It is so worthy of Him, and of what we have learned of His intention. Here it is—"all sorts and conditions of men". It is not only an endeavour to define the vast comprehensiveness of His care and pity, though it certainly is that. It is also a description of what the fellowship of Jesus Christ, into which we are called by the Gospel, has from the beginning been—just a blending of "all sorts and conditions of men" into a unity in which each retains his individuality while contributing himself to the cause which is great enough to transform all whom it embraces into personal conformity to Him who is their Lord and Leader.

The first group of the Master's men, each so entirely himself, yet each so entirely His, illustrates this. No two of them are the least alike so far as temperament and natural endowment are concerned. They are of all sorts and conditions. And none of them is either advanced or handicapped by what he happens to be in himself.

Here is one of whom practically nothing is recorded beyond a single word. No accomplishment of speech or action on his part is chronicled. He is not distinguished by any outstanding gift or ability. There's literally nothing

said of him (probably because there's nothing to say!)
beyond this designation. He was a *zealot!*

Alternatively he is referred to as the Canaanite, which is,
however, just the Hebraic form of the same Greek term.
It does not suggest, as some have thought, that he came
from Cana, and may therefore have had some connection
with the first miracle that Jesus wrought—nor, as others
have concluded, that he was not a Jew at all, but a des-
cendant of one of the tribes dwelling in Canaan before the
conquest under Joshua, and therefore among the first-fruits
of the Gentile world to be gathered to Christ.

This is just a description of Simon—the man as he was, a
man of intensity of feeling and urgency of action, an
ordinary man with an enthusiasm which was out of the
ordinary. Whatever he took up, he took up with earnestness and passion. He was a man capable of a great and
dynamic devotion; the kind of man who says: "This one
thing I do", whatever the thing is that has captured his
heart. Not necessarily a noisy, self-advertising man (zeal
is not an excess of vulgarity!), but a man who does not
take anything up that has not first taken him up, and
then he's all in it, "horse, foot and guns"; one who does
not know what slackness is, to whom half-heartedness is
in the nature of an offence to the cause in hand.

Simon the Zealot. It does not tell us much about him,
and yet it's surprising how much it does tell, and how
vividly it sets him forth for our emulation, until we cry:
"Would that all the Lord's people were zealots!" Not
only was this the type of man he was—the fact that he is
known as the Zealot (not simply the zealous) suggests that
he was in association with a number of others, banded
together for a specific purpose in the effort to achieve
which anything less than zeal could only be a disqualifica-
tion.

"The Zealots" was the name borne by a society of
patriotic Jews who bitterly resented the Roman yoke and

strove to liberate their nation from its bondage and all the evils and abuses consequent upon it. In every likelihood Simon belonged to them. Under one, Judas, they had broken out in open rebellion at the time when Jesus was a boy in Nazareth, about ten years of age. Their revolt was, of course, put down by Rome under Pilate, who mingled their blood with their sacrifices, with the inevitable consequence that their seething discontent was driven underground to nurse itself and gather strength for another rebellion later on.

They were patriots to a man, dreaming their dreams of a people liberated from the degradation of foreign tyranny and determining to bring them about if they had to die in the attempt. The Old Testament prophets fed their minds and fired their hearts, with their glowing vision of a nation prosperously established and victoriously carrying on its life and commerce under the rule and favour of God. They prayed for the peace of Jerusalem and were ready to implement their prayers by flinging themselves against Jerusalem's foes at any time. It goes without saying they were not individualists; "Who lives if Israel dies?" might well have been their motto. They had to overcome—even in propagating their zeal—the supreme and complacent indifference of the great mass of the people who were content to "make the best of things" and preferred peace at any price rather than the stirring up of trouble, which, of course, to any zealot was rankest heresy and only poured oil upon the flame of their passion and determination. The certain way to increase the enthusiasm of any real enthusiast in a true cause is to oppose him.

To this society of like-minded men Simon belonged when the Master's invitation to join the group reached him. How, we are not told, except that it is safe to assume that the Master had had His eye upon him for some time. Such an infusion of earnestness, lit up with vision, was just what the group needed.

There are some good people (at least it is to be hoped they're good!) who affect a kind of scornful apathy in regard to public questions which they think is a mark of their superiority to those who treat them with anything like seriousness and personal purpose. They even go to the length of persuading themselves that unintelligent aloofness is a hall-mark of true piety, unaware that it is actually the denial of it. They're under the delusion that it is religion which informs the sentiment they cherish, that so long as I'm saved the country can go to the devil for all I care! They look with suspicion on anyone who is keen and alert to take his citizen's responsibilities seriously and is enthusiastic for social reform.

Such would have seen in Simon just a man "mixed up in politics" playing a part in a dirty game, with possibly an axe of his own to grind, which only goes to show what an immense difference there is between their view and the Master's.

It is interesting, and certainly not illegitimate, to contemplate how Simon, his fiery zeal already engaged, came under the attraction of the Master. I think that the zealot in him recognised the zealot in Jesus. He saw Him at work, teaching and demonstrating the Kingdom of God; and said: "Here's a Man who believes what He says, who practises what He preaches. He's making immense sacrifices—anyone can see that—and if He goes on as He's doing, He'll make many more before He's done. He's utterly unsparing of Himself; there must be something in what He says." So he listened, and as he listened there came back to his mind old words from the Synagogue Readings: "The zeal of Thine House hath eaten me up"; "The zeal of the Lord of Hosts shall perform this"—His promise to Israel, which had come to mean so much to Simon and his friends. And it dawned upon him that this day the Scriptures were being fulfilled. The zealot took flame, and there and then he signed on for good and all. No half-measures for Simon.

Love answered to love without stammering or stuttering or making any reserves. From that hour Simon was "all in" with the Master. He couldn't do things by halves. A hundred per cent devotion was the only sort he was capable of and it's the only sort the Master has any use for.

And what of the Master? Did He show His sympathy with Simon's social passion, with the aims of the zealot, or did He stamp on them? It is a practical certainty that what won Simon was the fact that the Master's aims went so much further than his own—in the same direction! Much, very much, of His teaching was without meaning apart from a new social order. The abuses the zealots aimed to sweep away, the injustice they were determined should end, the tyranny they were banded together to destroy, the ideals for the nation they strove to secure— Simon recognised all this as being in the Master's programme. With him and his fellow-zealots, however, it meant only dreams and secret conclave and heated speeches and running necks into nooses. With him it meant a crusade, openly avowed, something to be set about at once, and something that went deeper and further and higher than their maximum thought.

They were all out for revolution, but here was One who knew more about revolution than they ever dreamed! And One who knew how to bring it about! One to whom revolution could only be accomplished in one way! And He knew the way and was doing more to promote it in a single day than the zealots had accomplished in all their years of plotting and scheming and propaganda, for while they were all for national revolt, He was for personal regeneration; while they saw Rome as the enemy, He saw sin.

So He convinced Simon, not so much by what He said, as by what He was, that there was a surer way to realise the zealot's passionately-pursued aims, and the Master began to bring his native ardour under the control of the highest consecration, and to gear his fervent enthusiasm to the highest tastes, and to use his individual loyalty, his whole-heartedness, his contagious enthusiasm, his dependable energies. How greatly He used them is His own secret.

I should not be greatly surprised if Simon's zeal more than once proved an embarrassment to some of the other members of the group ; for he was always ready, like David Livingstone, to go anywhere as long as it was forward and to do anything as long as it furthered the cause. He obliged them to keep up with him, and without doubt he was a pace-maker. Zeal and "safety first" have nothing in common. I can imagine circumstances where his energy tired them out and his abounding vitality depressed, because it condemned, them. There could be no hanging back where Simon was. Duty never lost its attractiveness to him! Every day was a new beginning with renewed strength. The fire never burned down! The lamp never dimmed—until his companions, forced to keep up with him, found themselves compelled to resort often to the Master in whose presence they wonderfully revived, and so came to bless the day that Simon the Zealot became one of them.

Of course he had much to learn. His impulsiveness and overeagerness time and again brought him, without doubt, under the Master's gentle but firm correction. His zeal doubtless ran away with him at times, and only those who have trodden it know how humiliating the way back can be. Further, his narrow provincialism, the outlook of a political Jew who could see no good thing out of Jewry— certainly not in a single Roman—had to be overcome. Prejudice and antipathies had to be lost, and a world-sympathy and a world-purpose acquired. But his zeal was a zeal to be the best he could be for the Master he had come to love better than life, and he did not flinch from the revolutionary changes and adjustments which the new life necessitated for him.

He knew the revolution had begun, because it had begun in him, and there was literally nothing he would not attempt and carry through if the Master indicated it as His desire, for what he did he did thoroughly. Zeal such as his does not exhaust itself by making beginnings only, as do those who are always keen on something, but never for long. The Master could absolutely depend on him. What a strength he must have been to Him—a man whose energy matched his faith, and a doer and not a talking cumberer of the ground.

By that time the revolution had proceeded quite a distance, for it was demonstrated, beyond cavil, that there is a power that can unify the world—man and man, class and class, nation and nation, race and race—and that it is actually at work winning its own opportunities.

It must have been strange, and a bit awkward at first, for two men like Simon and Matthew to find themselves together in the group, committed to the sharing of life in its most intimate aspects. One was an ex-member of the Roman Civil Service ; the other an implacable foe to everything Roman. Their views on many points were quite irreconcilable. If they were to live and work together they had each a lot of forgetting to do. Political animosity runs deep. It would be hard for a zealot to forgive and forget. Was the Master thinking specially of them when he said: "A new commandment . . . that ye love one another, as I have loved you"?

At any rate, they were actually reconciled to one another in Him. Hatred did turn to friendship ; bitterness did become brotherhood ; contempt did give place to comradeship. Simon the Zealot is of one accord, even with Matthew, after the Cross and their common experience of the Master's love when they meet to pray in the Upper Room, and as brothers to claim the Promise of the Master.

So much, at least, did this tireless, eager, intent, vital man contribute to the witness of the group to the reality of the Kingdom—by being himself. Would that all who claim to be of the Master's company were zealots.

The Christian Church today needs nothing so much as this. The average church member is zealous enough in business, in money-making, in achieving social progress, in seeking pleasure, in pursuing all sorts of personal aims, but when it comes to the actual thing the Church exists for, their dispositions seem to change; their energies certainly droop, their indifference is an effective drag upon the chariot-wheels of the Almighty; and together they actually bring the Church under the world's contempt as an effete, meaningless institution that has outlived its usefulness. They have put their own character upon it.

What the Master needs is the zeal which takes its faith in Him seriously because it takes Him seriously. People who press towards the mark, not dawdle towards it; who do the will of God, not merely assent to it; who sacrifice for the Cause, not simply sentimentalise about it; who are not lukewarm, but redhot; who don't patronise religion, still less play at it, but who are possessed by its realities and its urgencies. Before such a Church nothing hostile to its aims could stand.

You have the zeal, as witness your life in those other directions, in pursuit of those aims which have captured your interest. Let the Master have it, and baptise it into His service. Give Him His chance to interest you! For how much does He count with you? He "gave Himself for us, that He might redeem us from all iniquity, and purify unto Himself a people for a possession, zealous of good works". *Beware* lest, in the Great Day, Simon the Zealot should rise to condemn you for having received much and returned little, for having been much forgiven and for loving little, for having been zealous about the wrong things and indifferent to the claims of the Master who bought you with His Blood, for having been everyone's man but His.

VIII

BARTHOLOMEW

FROM the earliest times Bartholomew has always been identified with Nathanael, and all that we know of him is in the record of his meeting with the Master and what transpired between them. It is in the light in which all men st~nd revealed that we see all there is to be seen of one who played an inconspicuous part in the life of the group. His character is etched in a few bold lines, each of them as suggestive as it is definite. We are left in no manner of doubt as to yet another type of man welcomed by the Master into His fellowship, fitted for and used by Him in the work of the Kingdom.

The identification of Bartholomew with Nathanael rests upon a series of deductions, so lawful indeed, so unavoidable as to establish the fact, that in the story of that momentous interview we have actually the beginnings of an attachment that meant, for all time, life as the Master's man. Bartholomew is evidently a surname, like Barjona or Iscariot; just Bar-Tholmai. The Synoptists never mention Nathanael; John never mentions Bartholomew. As Bartholomew he appears in three lists next to Philip. What more natural, considering Philip's share in the bringing of him to Jesus? All those whose calling by Christ is recorded in John i (Philip, Andrew, Simon Peter) became members of the group. It is not likely that Nathanael should be an exception, the more so since the Master so highly commended him! After the Resurrection, when Jesus appeared to seven of the group on the sea-shore, their names are given, and one is Nathanael! We may leave it at that: Bartholomew and Nathanael are one.

Evidently a fisherman, whose home town was Cana of Galilee, he was a friend of Philip, who at once, upon making the great discovery about Jesus, set himself to win him also. To Philip's overflowing declaration he instinctively opposes both doubt and prejudice. That was the kind of man he was! The very mention of Nazareth roused him. That town had a sinister reputation, perhaps not entirely undeserved, when it is borne in mind how it treated its own Citizen, making the first of all the attempts on His life He suffered in three years. Possibly there were local rivalries between Nazareth and Cana—only five miles apart. Bartholomew is very suspicious and not a little contemptuous: "What! Nazareth! Can any good thing come from there? Impossible!" Obviously he was conservative also —to a fault, and apt to be a bit prejudiced, which is the danger of conservatism in any field. He was one of those who venerate the past, "the good old days", until they are unable to see any good in the present, or any hope in the future, and can only contemplate a change of any kind with a sniff. Who, that has ever had anything to do with progressive religion, that is with the religion of Christ, does not know those conservative sniffs which do duty for arguments, and make one utterly despair of their perpetrators? But unlike many of that order, Bartholomew's prejudice was not just sheer obstinacy. He might be critical, but he was not cynical. His doubts were not the voice of pride. His conservatism might be narrow, but it was open to conviction because it was sincere and free from anything like vested interest. His mind might be made up, but it was not closed.

Philip knew his man, and put up to him a proposition which he was quite sure he would not reject. "Come and see for yourself." There's always hope for a man who admits (if only to himself) the possibility that he may be

wrong and the other man right—a man who's not fooled
by his own fancied omniscience. Bartholomew came and
saw and was conquered. The fact is interesting and significant that before the Master said anything to him, He said
a great deal about him—in a very few words. For there
is no higher praise that can be bestowed on any man than
that on such authority he should be called "guileless, a
true man, an example of what all men should be and
would be, if they were determinedly true to the highest
loyalties they know; an Israelite indeed". For the guileless
man is the transparent man, the man who cherishes no
mixed motives, the man you must believe in even when
you can't agree with him and the exact opposite of the
man with whom you agree but in whom you can't believe.
Bartholomew was that kind! I quite expect he wasn't very
successful on the business side of the fishing-boat partnership—"a bit too simple, too easily taken in, too ready to
trust people". A man who never learnt the "tricks of the
trade" because he scorned them. The kind of man who,
when in Rome, always does what the Romans ought to do.
The sort of man who thought more of making his life than
his living. Not a "smart" man—thank God!—but clean
and dependable and utterly honest. A man who had all
along been quite unconsciously preparing himself for something bigger than he knew, and had this fine contribution
of character to carry over into the group-life of the Master's
men. He'll get a great reward one day, when the Master
makes up accounts and says: "Well done, good and faithful
Bartholomew!" But it won't be greater than the tribute
He paid to his moral quality that day.

It may well be that the 15th Psalm had been his model,
for it is evident that he approached its ideal. It was, in
any case, the outstanding characteristic of the man that
he took the things of the soul seriously. He had been
accustomed to withdraw from the cares and occupations
of his home and business and even from the services of the

Synagogue, to a quiet trysting-place in order to hold con-
verse with God and his own soul. No one knew where he
went, nor what he was doing. A man like Bartholomew,
to whom prayer and spiritual communion and the struggles
of the soul are realities, does not advertise them. But there,
under the fig-tree in some unfrequented garden shaded
from the hot Syrian sun (by night of course he would be
out on the lake, dipping and hauling the nets and helping
handle the boat, pulling his weight!), he came at grips
with the problems of his life, and groped after the Promises
of God and stretched out his hands to the Unseen.

How had it all begun with him? We do not know, but
from our own knowledge of ourselves we can almost reconstruct his experience. Was it that some cherished plans
went wrong and his life was flooded with disappointment?
Did his love miscarry and his heart break? Or was the
light of his life removed by pestilence? Had a succession
of bad catches brought him into serious straits—a man with
the support of others depending upon him? Or did a series
of sudden lake-storms carry away all his gear and batter
his boat until it was practically useless—and where's the
money for repairs to come from? Was it sheer dishearten-
ment that took him to the fig tree, a man for whom the
bottom had dropped out of things? Had his "own familiar
friend" whom he trusted turned out unworthy and repaid
his open-heartedness with treachery? Such things do happen!
Never so certainly as to the open-hearted, guileless, un-
suspecting, trustful man, who suffers intensely when the
poisoned points of disloyalty and hypocrisy pierce him. Or
had conscience been worsted in some secret conflict with
specious temptation? Had he given way where he should
have stood fast? Was he burdened with a sense of guilt and
defilement and the uselessness of starting afresh? Was his
self-confidence broken beyond repair? Had he had a glimpse
into his own heart and a peep into hell? Or had he come
under the spell of some old Prophetic word which had

opened up new worlds to him and had filled his heart with
vague longings after God? And had he found himself in
consequence misunderstood and desperately lonely amid
the polite indifference of those among whom he lived? Was
it for some such reason that he began to seek the Lord
while He might be found? Again, we do not know. But
this we do know, that all the time the Unsleeping Shepherd
of Israel was sharing his solitude, entering into his remorse,
his sorrow, his struggles, his hopes, and by means of them
was leading him to Himself. And when Jesus spoke, like
a flash the light burst upon Him! "When thou wast under
the fig-tree I saw thee!" The Master simply told Bartholomew what no one else could have told him about
himself. It was like the secret sign, the private password
of some Order of which they both were members! Like a
flash Bartholomew knew there was One who shared the
deep secret of his life; One who understood and sympathised
with him and was out to help him to realise the thing he
sought. And then the Master—intent on winning this man
to be one of His men—put Bartholomew's secret yearnings
into words of promise which, at once, expressed them as
he could never have done, and transcended them far
beyond his most fervid dreams.

On the instant Bartholomew knew what those secret
intimations of conscience, those uprisings of high resolve,
those calming visitations of peace, those inward urgings of
heart, those alternations of light and shadow—of ease and
concern—which he had known under the fig tree had all
meant! He had thought of himself as a seeker, but now
he knew there had been another more determined than
himself; and that He who had sought him in secret had
now claimed him openly and for ever. Here was One who
understood him. The old solitary loneliness of his life,
carefully hidden—even from Philip—was over! The key
to the mystery was, at last, in his hand! The uncertainties
of the future which he had feared had suddenly become

certainties he could rely on. From that hour he was the Master's man! They both realised they'd been made for each other—from the foundation of the world, and, unaccustomed to anything but frankness, Bartholomew there and then declared, before everyone, his newly born conviction: "Thou art the Son of God! Thou art the Messiah!"

He actually proclaimed the Master long before Peter did, and became the spiritual ancestor of that long line of men who have believed with the heart and confessed with the mouth the Lord Jesus, and have lived in the light and warmth of His salvation in every age! Away went his prejudices! And his contempt for Nazareth! And his conservatism! And his honest narrow-mindedness! He has found his Master, and the Master has found His man! And Bartholomew's staid heart is singing to the music of a promise which already he realises is bigger than he can see: "Thou shalt see greater things than these. . . . Heaven open, and the angels of God!" Not, mark you, "new things" but just things as they are and always have been. It is as though the Master said: "There always have been angels ascending and descending. It was they who carried up to the Throne the tidings of your struggles under the fig-tree. It was they who brought thence that consciousness of God you dimly enough realised there. Henceforth you shall be aware of them, and of the ladder on which they traffic. You shall see the Son of Man, your Saviour and Brother and Master, filling not Heaven alone but 'Heaven and earth', and making these twain one. Never again shall you feel yourself lost in a lost world! Even though you see only 'through a glass darkly', you shall see! And you shall see something that is actually there to be seen! And steadily your power to see the invisible shall strengthen, and your knowledge shall increase with it, until one day, you know, even as all along you have been known."

Little wonder that such implicit undertaking, backing such explicit understanding, captured Bartholomew, body

and soul; that he became, from that hour, one of the
Master's inseparables; that the rest of his days he devoted
to the service of declaring Him and of interpreting life to
the great world of the unconsciously redeemed though he
was apparently no preacher nor writer. Bartholomew was
of Cana! One sometimes wonders if there is any connection
between his enrolment as one of the Master's men and the
account, which immediately follows, of the Wedding and
the Miracle. Did he secure the invitation for the Master
and the group, and so make the connection between his
friends and their greatest Friend? And so declare himself? And so put them in the way of the Great Salvation?
Or was it in his own house that the marriage took place?
Was it, perhaps, his own? Was this the first thing he told
the Master in their first private talk—that he was betrothed,
and that his bride-to-be was like-minded, and that he must
bring her to see him? And was the Christ-graced Wedding
the outcome of the Master's talk with them both? And
did Bartholomew set up the first Christian home? And did
the Master first manifest His glory in that home, just as
He has been doing ever since wherever two disciples build
their nest in the True Vine? And was that—a Christian
home with all its splendid effluences—Bartholomew's great
contribution to the Kingdom? There is really none greater!

It will surprise no one but himself to find his name, the
name of a guileless, single-minded man, on one of the
Foundations of the City that lieth four-square in the day
when the top stone is laid with shoutings of "Grace, Grace
unto it"!

The Master is still served by men of ordinary capacity,
and dominating sincerity. He never needed them more
than now. It's up to you to supply His need as you fain
believe He has supplied yours.

IX

JOHN

WHEN one man is chosen from a group of like-minded men—each of them with his own distinctive personality, but each enrolled in the same cause, and each essential, in the eyes of the Master, to its accomplishment—and chosen for the close intimacy of a special friend, it is evident that there is more than caprice, far more than arbitrary favouritism, behind the choice.

It is one of the outstanding features of the records of the Master and His men that John occupied the primacy—not of leadership, natural gift, aptitude and zeal—but of friendly, human intercourse with the Master. In a special sense he was His friend; he was "the disciple whom Jesus loved". Plainly there was that in John which drew him and Jesus together into a quite unusual degree of mutual understanding, and appreciation. The Master had no favourites. No one of His men was favoured above another. What He said He said unto them all. No one of them was, in the slightest degree, handicapped by having anything withheld from him that was vital to his development or to his service. Yet temperament, capacity, natural bent, all played their part in determining each man's response to the Master's influence. The new content did not alter the old shape of the vessel. Certainly each one gave the Master a unique opportunity, and so, in turn, rendered the Cause a unique service.

In the case of John this is, perhaps, more obvious than in the case of others. But, distinctive though it be, John's example is not meant to deter or discourage any. It is, on the contrary, an assurance that each of us may be something quite uncopied and quite unmatched as one of the Master's men.

There is no uniformity of any kind which authenticates the living branches of the True Vine. But there is a unity of life-giving fellowship with the vine itself which actually makes each one essentially and particularly itself.

There is probably more data to hand for the formation of a sound judgment and characterisation of John than of any of the others in the group; for have we not the Book of the Revelation, the Fourth Gospel, and three Epistles? John came into contact with the Master, along with Andrew, through the witness of John the Baptist. From what we know of him we should hardly have thought that his somewhat shy, deep, reserved, strongly affectionate nature would have been attracted by the flaming Evangel of the rough desert-dweller. Perhaps, however, it was because he was a thoughtful man, a man who pondered upon life and its ways with particular reference to himself, that he listened to John's interpretation of the ancient Scriptures, its intensely modern application, and its inescapable corollary: "Repent"!

Upon his sensitive spirit such preaching brought a black cloud. He became aware of his shortcomings and his sins. Being as sincere as he was sensitive, he did not attempt to come to terms with his conscience in any less drastic and revolutionary way than that which the Prophet indicated. Sin was a thing to be repented of, confessed, and forsaken. His baptism at the hands of John, his namesake, meant this for him. It was the most serious hour of his life. Henceforward he "loved righteousness and hated iniquity" with an intensity which is unmistakably characteristic of every bit of writing that bears his name. And it was just then, when the fire had begun to burn, that the Master found him, and found in him a loyal follower and an understanding friend. With Andrew, he shared the amazing wonder of a night's sojourn with the Master, and learned then what formed the foundation of life-long admiration and devotion. Heaven opened for John that night. From that night onward to the end—a further distance for him than for any others of the group; for he out-lived them all —his sun no more went down, neither did his moon withdraw its light. From that very hour the Master became his everlasting light, and life was indissolubly bound up with Him. How much history started that night! How much history always does start when a man—any man— becomes the Master's man!

The records of the group do not contain anything outstanding in the part John played. Beyond the fact that he shared the experience of the three—joining Peter and his brother James in attendance upon the Master on the Mount of Transfiguration, in the house of death and mourning, and in the Garden of Temptation—nothing is told of him except the incident at the Supper, when love took him deeper into the Master's counsels than any of the others; and the incident at the Cross, when the Master committed the care of His mother to the only one of the group that had not forsaken Him; and the incident beyond the Resurrection, when love recognised the Master in the morning's grey mist on the seashore. But these incidents are enough to convince us of the man John was. Modestly, he always refers to himself, when it is necessary to do so, in an indirect way. He is either "that disciple", or "this man", or "the disciple whom Jesus loved". Not that he even hints at a special measure of the Master's affection above that bestowed on others. He is so lost in wonder that Christ could love such a one as he, that the sheer marvel of it captured his mind. It is his only boast that the Master loves him, with the love that covers a multitude of sins. But these incidents show that he, too, was a man who loved because he was loved. He was, pre-eminently, the disciple who loved Jesus. He may suppress his own

name, for it is a way love has to want all the attention
and admiration and glory for the loved one and never
for itself, but all the same we know him as the man who
served by loving. And we are grateful to him for showing
us how, too, we may serve, and for reminding us that,
in loving, there is only one thing we have to watch ; that
is, not the measure but the quality of our love, that our
love is not in word nor in tongue, but in "deed and in
truth". Those are his very words.

Of course, John was not a soft, effeminate, sentimental
type, the sort of man who walks delicately, speaks minc-
ingly, thrills emotionally, and disgusts other men by his
affectations. That type of thing is not love. Love is a
thing that has iron in its blood and strength in its hands
and feet; true love has energy in its mind and courage
in its heart. And loyalty that takes no thought of cost is
the breath of its life. Jesus would never have called John
"Boanerges" if he had had no backbone. For that term
signified with him (as also with his fisherman brother) a
man of determination and enthusiasm; a man of directness
in purpose and in aim; a man unafraid and undaunted;
a man of personality, who would carry his full count in
any company. A man is not less a man because he loves;
he is all the more a man. It is "the Man Christ Jesus"
that draws out the man John and grapples him to Himself
with hooks of steel. And John (unlike some modern
Christians, who must attract attention to themselves or
suffer) does not vulgarise his love by parading it, nor dilute
it by talking of it.

From the beginning John was something of a mystic,
which is, by the way, far removed from being unpractical.
Indeed, it is the mystics who, in carrying out human relationships, are the most practical people in the world;
for they see in others what is hidden from ordinary sight,
and act on what they see. He was a fisherman, acquainted
with nature in all her moods, accustomed to look beyond

the storm and the glassy calm, the crimson sunset and the scudding clouds and the fierce lake-storms, to what lay there; accustomed to meditate upon God; and to cultivate the kingdom of his mind. John was a man of reverence, which is not a quality of small natures, but of great. He was a good listener, both to nature, to the Baptist, and to the Master. He was a careful observer who did not lose the finds of his observation by failing to hide them in his heart. But above all he was a child-like, gentle man, with that gentleness which is the truest expression of strength.

And he was modest withal; and unenvious; and unresentful; a lover of men because a lover of the Master. John was one who could rejoice in the importance of others without cherishing jealousy of them—a rare virtue—as witness in all the records: "James and John", "Peter and John". The glory of the second place more than satisfied him; he knew it was more than he deserved. His love for the Master was quite unquestioning as to His placing of him. John knew his times were in Christ's hand, and he was more than content they should be there. So long as he could serve the Lord Jesus and support Him, so long as he could be with Him, quietly, unobtrusively ministering to Him, nothing else mattered. Is it to be wondered at that the Master should choose such an one for His friend or that He should beckon him to the place next Himself at the Supper? Love like John's is a pearl of great price to Jesus Christ, the Lord.

After the Crucifixion, and the Resurrection and the Day of Pentecost, we see John giving evidence by his boldness that he had "been with Jesus", and by his self-effacing modesty and large-heartedness that he had drunk deeply of His Spirit. He is more than ever the Master's man now that He has gone, and now that it costs heavily to maintain loyalty to Him—and may, at any time, cost any man his life. Silently he slips out of the picture of the Early Church's life and extension, in which evidently he played a full part.

But not by any self-endeavours did this apostle serve, for he recalls (he alone reports it) that the Master had said: "I live by the Father", and has learned that his own powers were insufficient. Jesus Christ literally lived in him.

The Master takes him behind the scenes, by way of an exile in Patmos, a banishment to the convict-settlement where prisoners, chained to their wheelbarrows and to one another, worked under the lash in the marble mines. There he wrote what he saw—the Book of the Revelation, the Vision of the Over-Ruling Providence and of the Eternal Glory that was to hearten his fellow-believers in the trials and persecutions which were, even then, upon them, and in the great cataclysm of the nations which was at hand and in which they would inevitably be involved.

How unaffectedly humble, how simply modest he is, in setting forth what he saw! He claims no superior wisdom (unlike many who from time to time take in hand to interpret what he wrote!). He is just "your brother and companion in tribulation and in the Kingdom and patience of Jesus". And in reading the book the writer is the last person anyone would think of; which is as he would have it, for it is the Revelation—not of "John the Divine", but of "Jesus Christ"—of Jesus Christ in His, as yet, undiscovered fulness of Grace and Truth and Power.

Later on he writes, probably at the request of those to whom he often spoke of Him, his memoirs of the Master. By that time he was the last of those who had companied with Him. The three Synoptic Gospels were already in existence, and the facts of Christ they set forth needed to be supplemented. Matthew, Mark and Luke had related what they had seen and heard concerning Him. John knew Him as they did not, and he put down—in what is incomparably the greatest literature of all time—just what had impressed him ; most of it entirely unreported by the others.

The Gospel bears revealing traces of the writer—the ex-fisherman, and intimate friend, and now the old man with an ever-young heart, as constant to the Master as in the days of long ago. Still unobtrusive, he never mentions his own name in it. In order not to speak of himself he actually omits to record the incidents in which he himself figured—content to leave them to the other writers. What they have said is enough; until some of the Higher Critics (literally unable to see the wood for the trees!), to whom his reticence only spells ignorance, declare that John could never have written the Gospel; and refer to "the writer of the Fourth Gospel". Such is the wisdom of this world!

He tells of the Master in a series of personal encounters and interviews, details of which he could have only obtained from Him; as, for example, with Nathanael, and Nicodemus, and the woman at the well-side. And he alone records some of His most priceless sayings—as they had gripped him—about the New Birth, and the "whosoever" of the Gospel, the assuring "him that cometh unto Me", the Good Shepherd and the True Vine, the Living Water, the Eating of His Flesh and Drinking of His Blood, and the Holy Spirit promises.

Anyone taking up his Gospel soon forgets the human writer—as he would have wished. The glory of the Master obliterates all else. And this is what John's unmixed love always wanted—to introduce men to Him. As witness the three Epistles he also wrote—each directed to the same end, "that ye also may have fellowship"—the fellowship that has changed existence into life for him.

There, too, the utter simplicity of love and love's beliefs and confidences are seen. He's an old man now. But his eye is not dim, even if his natural force is abated. And this is what he sees—as the epitome of all he learnt from the Master—and is still learning: that God is love. He learnt it from the Master, and he has proved it in life, that the whole duty of man is to love Him and His. Heaven itself is only the fruition of that life.

Tradition says that the apostle in his old age was carried into church at Ephesus every Lord's Day, just to say: "Little children, love one another." Questioned as to its constant reiteration, the old man could only reply: "Because this is the Lord's sole command. If we fulfil this there's nothing more to be done."

That is one of the Master's men, who loved because he was first loved; and fulfilled his love in life and his life in love. Which is beyond none of us—since the Redeeming, Transforming Love is unchanged.

The Master still wants men—to be with Him and that He may send them forth. Will you be one?

X

JUDAS ISCARIOT

O F ALL the men who came into revealing association with the Master, Judas Iscariot is perhaps the most striking and certainly not the least interesting. For while he began in the clear light of morning to company with Him and with His, his career ended in the blackness of a starless midnight. His name stands for perfidy, for treachery, for the most damning and damnable of all sins —the betrayal of a trustful friend. So that, even to this day, to liken a man to Judas is to put the greatest possible dishonour upon him. Men will consort with flagrantly bad men, with men whose weakness or whose circumstances, or both, have brought them within the displeasure of Society and the meshes of the Law, and will make allowances for them and succeed in finding some good in them. But no man wants to be a friend of a Judas-man! His is the unforgivable sin. A leprosy of shame clings to him. Contempt is the only feeling that ordinarily decent men can have for him. By every rule of human association he has put himself outside the pale.

Everyone knows that behind the particular act that earned for him that title of infamy there lies a story of base ingratitude and sly selfishness and slimy falseness, masked by hateful hypocrisy and nauseating cant. With such evil significance has Judas filled a once honourable name! For the name was not always despised and abhorred —Judas Maccabeus, for example, was one of the greatest and truest Hebrew patriots. Judas the brother of Jesus, too, bore the name without attaching any sinister meaning to it. But this Judas, one of the Master's chosen men, dragged it in the mire, degraded it beyond the lowest; until there is no name so surrounded with loathing. And the mother is not yet born who would ever allow her child to be christened Judas!

And yet no man in the group had any more promising start than Judas. Although we know nothing of the actual event of his calling by the Master, what experiences led up to it, what influences had been at work urging him to link up with Jesus and the new movement, it is quite evident that Judas was entirely sincere. There is no evidence at all that he was, from the first, a self-seeking hypocrite. Nor that the Master who, it must be remembered, spent a whole night in prayer before choosing the Twelve, had made any mistake in including him. On the contrary, it is fair to assume that he was moved by a blameless and noble enthusiasm when (as a man with some experience of affairs, for was he not made the group treasurer?) he made that renunciation which all must make who would join the Master and which to others must have seemed like madness. Conviction and eager courage voiced a faith which was bright with the bloom of freshness and eagerness. Judas was as much in earnest, and as disinterested, in joining the group as any of the others.

The only handicap upon his intentions was the same handicap which each carried—his own nature, with which constant contact with the Master was calculated to deal effectively, to reduce it from a disability to a positive capacity. In the case of all the others this actually happened. They became increasingly competent for the carrying out of His bidding, by becoming increasingly of one mind and purpose with Him. Judas grew steadily worse, until in the end "Satan entered into him" through a door which he himself opened! He became blinded to all his vows and recreant to all his experiences and disloyal to all his benefits. He made a calculated bargain with the Master's

enemies to betray Him into their power for a paltry price.
He feigned a friendship he no longer felt, and actually
kissed the Master whose downfall he was profitably assist-
ing in. He became the victim of unavailing remorse and
of unsatisfying success; and by his own hand "went to his
own place" (to carry out the eternal destiny for which he
had fitted himself) unattended except by stinging, scorching, mocking memories and regrets! And of him the Master
said: "it had been good for that man had he not been
born!"

> For ships sail East, and ships sail West
> On the self-same winds that blow.
> It is not the gale, but the set of the sail
> That determines the way they go!

It's really a terrifying story, for what happened to him
might happen to any of us. Privilege evidently does not
ensure men against ultimate disaster. The same kind of
tragedy may be re-forming in any life, as witness the
startled question of the other men in the group when the
Master said: "One of you shall betray Me"—a question
which voiced a wholesome misgiving: "Lord, is it I?"
Let no one settle down to a self-complacent survey of Judas,
as though they themselves are remote from all possibility
of such undetected instabilities as brought about his ruin.
"Let him that thinketh he standeth take heed lest he fall."

How did it all begin? And how did it go on as it did
under the influence and the eye of the Master, and the
protective activities of the life of His men together? Well,
it all began by Judas failing to make an entire surrender
of himself to the Master at the start. He simply didn't leave
all when he joined Him. He carried over into the new life
part of the old love, which right from the start disputed the
Master's absolute rule, and finally repudiated it entirely.
Judas was a mercenary-minded man, and always had been;
the kind of man of whom it is said "he's keen"—meaning

thereby keen on making money. He had what is called "an
eye for the main chance", but, like most men of that ilk,
he didn't know what the Main Chance really is! He thought
it was money and so became "penny-wise and soul-foolish"!
And even though he was continually hearing so much from
the Master about such folly (hearing without learning!) he
let money exercise its fatal charm upon him, until he'd do
anything (and anybody!) for it—without it ever dawning
upon him that he was vainly trying to do what the Master
said was impossible—to serve God and Mammon. All of
which is not to suggest that he was a deliberately bad man,
only that he was a "double-minded man". He simply did
not let his new allegiance dislodge the old supremacy. He
did not yield to the Master the whole area of life. He con-
sented (with himself) to be only partly "spiritual"! And
the old nature—which is always the battleground of the
new life—asserted itself, until Judas just couldn't understand how the Master could be so indifferent to money,
and all that it brings, and to rich men whom He seemed
to antagonise with so little respect! Until, indeed, he
honestly felt that Jesus and His unworldly group really
needed someone "with a head on his shoulders" to look
after their interests, and actually persuaded himself that
he was that Heaven-sent protection! As witness, when a
poor woman poured her treasured ointment in fragrant
devotion upon the Master's feet, his protest: "It might
have been sold for 300 pence!"

Slowly and insidiously he came entirely under the power
of the thing he really loved most. Temptation made successful appeal to latent cupidity. Zeal for the unselfish ideals
of the Master began to flag as greed gradually took over
control of his soul. Covetousness got the better of piety.
Moral corrosion set in. A few pence, taken now and again
from the bag, fed the flame of his money-lust, which cul-
minated in his acceptance of the High Priest's thirty pieces
of silver. He was overcome just because his allegiance,

openly professed, was secretly divided; just because he wasn't whole-hearted. Sincere as far as he went, he didn't go far enough! No one suspected him of dishonest action or of disloyal intention. He was certainly able to keep up appearances right to the end. At the Supper, with the thirty pieces of silver in his pocket weighing him down like thirty pieces of lead, he was yet able to sit near enough to the Master to dip his bread into the same dish. And, later, Judas came quite naturally up to Him to give Him the perfidious kiss!

And what about the Master, who knew well what was going on in the soul of the one He had chosen? Did He do nothing to save him from himself? It would seem as though He did everything possible to discover Judas to himself; to draw him out in self-confession of his tendencies and fears, and into closer intimacy with Himself who could have done wonders to help him overcome the money-menace which threatened and ultimately managed to destroy him. Think of the simply tremendous things He said about it—things which could only have concerned Judas, of all the group—about the tragedy of bursting barns and an insecure soul; about the disaster of a world gained and a life lost; about being aware of the blight of covetousness; about the abject folly of laying up for oneself earthly riches. Until it actually appears as though the Master had had him in mind more than all the rest! Judas must, many a time, have been afraid to catch the Master's eye. And it does not surprise us that, as the end drew near, "Jesus was troubled in spirit" at the thought that one of His men could be treacherous and betray His confidence. One can almost hear Him, in the solitude of His prayer-place, repeating the old Psalm: "Mine own familiar friend in whom I trusted, who did eat of my bread hath lifted up his heel against me. We took sweet counsel together and walked in the House of God as friends!" And again turning from this bitterness to His unfailing refuge!

What would not have happened if Judas had only taken his misgivings, in secret, to the Master! If he had just told Him that he had a foe that was too strong for him! If only he had opened his heart as readily to Him as he was opening it to the demon of greed and avarice! But no! He was in love with the foe! His idol had become his ideal! His heart had never been wholly the Master's, and every day its divided, contending loyalties were more evident and more unreconcilable.

Even to the last the Master endeavoured to make him face up to himself. At the Table He gives him the sop! In the Garden He calls him "Friend" and does not resist his treacherous kiss! It was a last endeavour to win him back to his first intention! But it failed! The poor, possessed man violently wrenches himself from the kindly grasp of love, and takes the mad plunge! When the raging fever cooled to disillusion and despair, his too-late confession: "I have sinned", completely exonerated the Master! He had done His utmost (and Judas knew it) to save him.

It has been ingeniously suggested that Judas was not simply out for personal gain in betraying Christ. That he was moved by vehement zeal to force Him to declare Himself a king! That he resented Christ's unbusinesslike way of going about things, and so manœuvred to put Him into a position from which He could only extricate Himself by a spectacular and convincing miracle! That he was merely trying to speed-up the establishment of the Kingdom, to the service of which he had pledged himself! It has even been suggested that this idea of his was reinforced by his jealousy of the favoured Three—possibly of the entire eleven. They were all Galileans; he was from Kerioth in south-east Judea, a stranger among them and made to feel his position by them! He would establish himself, by a stroke of cleverness, as the Master's truest friend, the leader of the group. All very ingenious, but all such attempts favourably to assess his moral motives are entirely precluded by the records, and in particular by what the Master said of him! He never hinted at the possibility that Judas may have been just a well-meaning blunderer! What he said was: "One of you is a devil!" "It had been better for him that he had not been born!" And he said it with a sob in His voice!

What a warning flare is this story of one of the Master's men—a flare whose warning none of us dare disregard. If we do, it is at our peril. For unhappily there is nothing very exceptional in a divided heart, on the part of those who profess the faith of Christ. Judas only did what many another does—and seems to get away with. For how many give Christ less than the whole of their lives? How many have a love which contests His? In the bright light of reality how many are self-revealed as the slaves of this world, and its tinsel baubles and its deceiving riches? How many are actually robbing the Master whom they acclaim as Judas did?

When one sees what some titular Christians will do for money and its equivalents; how they will sell their good name; how they will lie; how they will deny their loyalties; how they will outrage the honour of the Christian Church; how they will pilfer from the bag (not by taking but by withholding), spending more on a single item of self-interest than their total givings to God's work in a year, more on entertainments and self-indulgence, on unnecessary adornment and attire than on the cause of God (so much so, indeed, as to make it impossible for them to give proportionately, not to say adequately, to the work of the Gospel); how they will content themselves to be in debt to God for unpaid tithes, a debt they never intend to discharge—for the idea of giving away a "tithe" they deride as absurd quixotism (whereas it isn't even good Judaism, much less Christianity, to give God less!)—when one sees this (and one does see it on every hand) one knows only too unmistakably that some people are flirting with spiritual disaster, as Judas did! That they're trifling with Christ and their own soul! That they're at the old Judas game of trying to make the best of both worlds! The game in which conscience is opposed by expediency, and choices are made between gain and godliness, and destinies are determined. For:

Still as of old, men by themselves are priced.
For thirty pieces Judas sold himself—not Christ!

Beware, my friends, of the small beginnings of great tragedies, in which the Master is betrayed into the hands of His enemies, and the betrayer—like Judas, is utterly fooled! Beware of the half-hearted Christian life which can only end in whole-hearted and destructive allegiance to the "god of this world"! Beware of the pitiful disaster of honouring the Master with your lips while your heart is actually given to another!

Of course the question will be asked: "Why did the Master ever choose such a man as Judas?" Until a yet more searching question simply clamours for answer: "Why did He choose me?" And the answer is, in both cases, the same—not for what he was! Certainly not for what he became! But for what he might have become! And the resolute prayer voices itself that the Master's verdict may never be "it had been good for that man if he had not been born"; but rather "it has been good for the world that he was born out of due time". For out of him, into its desert wastes, rivers of redemptive influence have flowed. And men call Me "Master" because they knew him as My man!

XI

THE TWO UNKNOWN

N OT ALL the stars in the Heavens are stars of the first magnitude. Thousands of nameless, twinkling points of light contribute to the glory of a perfect night. While Venus and Saturn and Jupiter and Mars and Uranus and the Great Bear and the Plough and Arcturus establish themselves in our minds as the major constellations by their outshining brightness, they would by themselves form a very different sky-view from that which gives them their setting. It is the myriads of the less-known and unknown shining worlds which combine with them in declaring the glory of God, that give to the Heavens their nightly beauty. Were it not for them, darkness would reign almost unchallenged from nightfall to sunrise. So, too, is it among those who turn many to righteousness and "shine as the stars for ever and ever". "One star differeth from another star in glory"—but all are stars! And He who lighted them "calls them all by name"!

Among the Master's men were two, of whom practically nothing is known beyond their names; though of whom a good deal that is of interest, and indeed of importance, to ourselves may be deduced and inferred. One is James, the Son of Alphaeus (called James the Less; not in contrast to the other James in relative importance, but descriptively—he was evidently a little man). The other is variously called Lebbæus, Thaddæus and Judas, the two former being obviously Greek forms of the Hebrew Judas or Jude. It would appear that they were brothers, like

James and John, and that they had a godly mother named
Mary. For she is specially mentioned as "the mother of
James" among those who ventured near to the Cross on
Calvary. It may be that she was the first in that family
to come into contact with the Lord Jesus, and under His
influence. What more likely—as every Christian mother
knows—than that she should desire for her two boys the
indescribable blessing that had come to her? That she
should herself introduce them to the Master when, impelled
not only by what she said to them but by what her
marvellously changed life told of His power, they came
to where He was? And that they, already convinced,
should themselves come under the spell of His personality,
and become the friends of their mother's new-found Friend,
soon to be invited also to join the group and to become
of the company of His men? Happy the sons that have
such a mother! Happy the mother that has such sons!

Parents—who would do anything, make any sacrifices,
to secure the best interests of your children—have you
made any serious efforts to bring them to Christ? Have
you given them any such cause to want to know Him as
it seems likely Mary gave to James and Thaddæus? Will
they be able at the Great Day to reproach you: "Mother,
Father, why did you never tell me what I must do to be
saved, and what to do with my now-wasted life?" You
give them the best start in life you can, send them to the
best school you can afford, give them every educational
and social advantage within your power, but have you
ever seriously set about compassing their conversion to
Christ? Have you given them cause to know that you
cherish for them the loftiest ambitions—not for riches,
honours, great names or high places, but higher far beyond
all such aims, the honour of being the Master's men? In
this life we get what we aim at if we aim properly—if we
want it sufficiently to pray and labour and sacrifice ourselves for it. It will be our eternal condemnation if our

desires for our children have been lower than this, and if the ordering of our lives has not implemented our desires!

But now to James and his brother Thaddæus. Literally nothing is known of them, beyond the fact that one of them put to the Master that question which evoked one of His most wonderful words: "Lord, how is it that Thou wilt manifest Thyself to us and not to the world?" For the query of "Judas, not Iscariot", was answered by that great saying—one of the Master's greatest—"If a man love Me he will keep My words, and My Father will love him and We will come unto him and make Our abode with him." Apart from that significant incident they are mere names, but names immortalised by their relationship to the Lord Jesus. Nothing they ever said or did is recorded. They seem to have been just obscure nobodies, men of no outstanding gift, with nothing to distinguish them, except their downright loyalty to the Master.

Often such "unknowns" (as they were), in any company, develop an inferiority complex. They belittle themselves and deprecate their own capacity, and tacitly accept the superficial judgment of onlookers that they are really of no account. There is no hint given that these two did. True, there is nothing said of their work. No striking advances of the Kingdom are credited to their initiative or their courage, but that is no warrant for concluding that they were any less useful to the Master, that they meant less to Him than the more prominent members of the group. Rather the absence of record suggests that they were just the type of man you can take for granted. Whoever else may fluctuate and falter, flourishing today and fading out of the picture tomorrow, they may be depended upon. Steady men; reliable; plodders (never plotters for some self-glory, which peril even the foremost members of the group did not always avoid!); men of the unwearied foot because men of the far, long look; men of dependable fidelity; men whose lives—humble, patient, quietly determined—help to keep the moral average up in the Church and the community; men who, if charged to give some account of themselves, would say with entire lack of self-consciousness (adapting the poet's lines):

> I live for Him who loves me,
> For Him who holds me true,
> For the Heaven that bends above me,
> For the good that I can do;
> For the wrong that needs resistance,
> For the cause that lacks assistance,
> For the future in the distance,
> And the good that I can do!

It was upon such men, equally with those of more striking quality, that the Master leant the weight of the work of His Kingdom, at its beginnings. What encouragement there is for us in the Apostleship of the two unknown! For although we have no record of what they did, it is certain that they served His Will. Otherwise there would at least be some mention of their rebuke by Him. But there is none. Had they failed, gone down before the immensity of the task (so entirely out of keeping with their own little-ness and inconsequence), deserted through sheer fright, depend upon it, we should have been told—for our own warning. And some other things may safely be assumed regarding them. They must have been splendidly free from jealousy, beautifully unenvious of their colleagues who, in one way or another, were more in the public eye! Their devotion to the Master was not marred, nor their service blighted, by self-pity over wounded self-esteem. They were neither irritated nor vexed by being passed over when it came to the seemingly more important and privi-leged tasks. They had no vulgar and vulgarising greed for applause. "Content to fill a little space" if the Master were thereby best served by them.

They may not have been faultless. None of the Master's men in that day was, nor in this day! But I believe they were blameless, their loyalty unaffected by their obscurity. And I believe, too, that their presence in the life of the group tended to keep things sweet among men who could get "on edge" with each other—and even with the Master at times. I believe that the contentment of James and Thaddæus was sometimes a rebuke, and always a benediction, to their companions. They may not have exerted a great deal of influence by anything they were capable of doing, but it's certain they were of the sort who exhale an unconscious, indefinable influence, under which others are restrained, or heartened and encouraged and set to longing that they might themselves be better men. To praying, too, and to determining, and to inward watching over their own inconsistencies and to repairing to the Master for more of His Spirit. Until one wonders what that group of men would have been without those two unknown, outshone, "back-row" men! What a heartening reflection for us this fact is: that splendid work, which never secures the recognition it deserves, which never brings those responsible for it into public notice, may be done, and is done, by inconspicuous, unimportant, quite ordinary people like ourselves!

In one of the most beautiful church buildings in the world—the College Chapel of King's, Cambridge, there is surpassingly lovely carving in stone and wood ornamentation scattered prodigally upon the perpendicular Gothic which literally makes the unique character of the place. Everywhere it meets and charms the eye. Nobody knows who did it! Hundreds of unnamed craftsmen must have given of their best. The founders, architect, builder of the great organ, all these are known. But, worthy of equal glory with the highest of them all, the workers in wood and stone are unrecorded. Their work alone tells their story. So is it in the work of the Kingdom in the world. Much of its best and most beautiful work is done by "the nobodies"—the men and women who love Christ and are filled with His Spirit, and carry out, in their lives, His precepts and so adorn the doctrine.

We sometimes hear the question debated: "Who won the war?" And some say—not without irony—the statesmen! Others, with strange lack of humour—or is it with over-plus of sardonic humour?—say the generals and admirals, and army of brass-hats! Some affirm it was the Press and its powerful propaganda, and others declare it was the inventors of tanks and other devilish engines of destruction. But every one knows that if the war was won, it was won by tens of thousands of anonymous nobodies! By splendid young subalterns, and company commanders, and men who actually lost their personal identity and became mere numbers—"Tommies"! Whatever was won, they won and paid for! So is it in the warfare by which the Kingdom comes. It is not the high ecclesiastics, great preachers, platform orators, conference leaders and committee men who win Christ's victories and souls to His allegiance. But the rank and file Christians! Successors of James-the-less and Thaddæus. The people who are not known, nor quoted, nor consulted, nor recognised. The ordinary, average, commonplace people who are like light and salt in the community. Not that the highly-placed are to be despised or under-valued. Far from it. We are glad to have them, and sometimes are even proud of them when they overstep the conventional restrictions of their office and forget themselves! But I sometimes think that it is, in the Kingdom, pretty much as it is in the world of nature. The really indispensables there are not the bewildering wonders, the high mountains and deep ravines and great waterfalls and massive sea-cliffs. They are the common things like air, and water and sunlight and the soil itself. For without these there is no life.

To come back to our "two unknown" among the Master's

men. James and Thaddæus did share a high commendation with the entire group: "Ye have continued with Me in My temptations!" Whatever else they may have lacked, however deficient in gift and capacity, they were men who had the courage and tenacity to stick out a hard thing! The Master had called them "to be with Him" and "with Him" they were and intended to be to the end.

Did the Master mean them—and others like them—when He said: "Many that are last shall be first"? And when He said that those who gave cups of cold water in His Name should, one day, be rewarded? Yes! He meant them and us! And He thought sufficiently highly of them to put their names upon two of the City's Foundation Stones! Which is to say that He knows the work of His unknown friends, and the worth of it, and that "the righteous", whatever place they fill in the scheme of things now (so long as they do fill it!), "shall be had in everlasting remembrance"!

When the work of earth is seen in its eternal projection this will be our amazement—the thrill of which we shall not lose through all the eternal days—that the Master should, all the time, have been making so much of our simple loyalty to Him. And "lost in wonder, love and praise" we'll exclaim with James and Thaddæus (our own forefathers in the Faith): "Who'd have thought it possible?"

Don't make it impossible by holding back from the Master now!

XII

THOMAS

O F ALL the Master's men, Thomas is the one to whom least justice is commonly done. He is, in fact, mostly known for what are felt to be his faults. When his name is mentioned it is usually as "doubting Thomas" that he is identified. As such he might be held in a certain degree of wondering disrespect, not to say contempt, had not the Resurrection story, in which he and the Master figure together, been chronicled. For it is a story, an epic, of the Master's fine insight, of His sympathy and understanding, and of His power to change the shadow of death into morning light for an honestly perplexed and sincerely purposed man whose faith, when it most needed to be at its brightest and best, was actually in eclipse. It is a picture in three colours—of doubt, disorder and deliverance. And, like all the records, the story is told and the picture drawn, not simply that we may benefit by being made aware of the reaction of a not uncommon temperament to the consistent influences of the Risen Master, but that we may be encouraged ourselves to draw near to Him for our own enlightenment and enduement for His service.

To appreciate the story, and its implications to ourselves, it is necessary to recall the kind of man Thomas was, to reconstruct his personality from the available data.

The first three Gospels tell nothing whatever about him, beyond the mere announcement of his name as "one of the Twelve". He is called by them all "Didymus", which simply means "a twin". And it has been conjectured, from the fact that in the Synoptists' lists of the Apostles his name is always coupled with Matthew's, that he and Matthew the publican were twin brothers. But there is nothing to support such a view, and, even if it were so, there could be no importance attaching to the relationship, since, when it comes to the ultimate values of life, "every man shall give account of himself"! Nothing is known of his conversion to Christ; nor of the influences that impelled him to follow his awakened interest; nor of what it was that awakened that interest; nor of the circumstances in which he came to join the group. Nothing at all! When we first meet Thomas he is already one of the Master's men.

But John, the writer of insight and intuition (as distinguished from the mere historian), tells us enough about Thomas to enable us to see the abiding significance and inwardness of the Resurrection incident in which he is so prominent. And what he tells of him is in the nature of attempt to set forth, in terms of life, what he has already said elsewhere in other terms—that there are Twelve Gates into the City of God; that Thomas has his own gate (which, as a matter of fact, every man must have) and that it is as beautiful a gate as that of any other citizen. For like every other Gate his gate, too, is a pearl! What kind of man then, was Thomas?

Evidently he was a man of slow mind: "Not o'er quick in the uptake!" A man who had to look all round any subject before he could pronounce upon it. A man with a somewhat melancholic habit, prone to see the dark side of anything, and rather to suspect it if it hadn't got a dark side. A cautious man, without much humour (probably with none, poor fellow!) who was apt to overdo the caution. A man who was a bigger worry to himself than to anyone else. A man of moods, attracted rather by the shadow than by the sunshine. A man who (if he had a favourite text, it was "prove all things") found it difficult to commit himself.

Thomas was a man who wouldn't sign on the dotted line until he had read and re-read the document. Faith came hard to him. Not that he distrusted people, but that he simply had to go slow with them until he knew, beyond question, that they were trustworthy. He had a questioning mind which was as much part of him as anything else in his make-up. He couldn't help it, and isn't to be blamed for it! Not the kind of man to be over-enthusiastic about anything; rather to be a bit distrustful of windy enthusiasm —especially in religious people, about Religion. The kind of man to whom life is a serious business—not to say a solemn business, and who makes a practise of watching his step. The sort of person to whom new ideas are not over-welcome, but by whom once received they are accorded tenacious fidelity. A really dependable man when you've got him. And Christ got him! Through all the days of his fellowship with the Master this temperament of his, with its characteristic brooding pessimism, was under the transforming discipline of His creative care. Out of this raw material, this stiffish clay, He, the great Artificer, produced the man we know Thomas actually became.

Two incidents show the true quality of the man deeper than any temperamental characteristics. The Master proposes to go into Judea. Lazarus is sick. His anxious sisters have summoned Him. The glory of God is at issue. The group, knowing the risks He ran in going into that district, tried to dissuade Him (not, unlikely, having some care as to their own safety!). All but Thomas, who said: "Let us go that we may die with Him!" True to form, he saw that nothing but death could come of this hazardous business. There could only be one end to this quixotic mission. But (and here is the bravery of the man who is ready to "go over the top" knowing what is over the top!) he means to go to death with the Master. Whatever his misgivings—and they're more than misgivings, they're certainties!—he has no intention of deserting. The deepest-down thing in Thomas is not doubt but love, that laughs at dangers. One can almost hear the other members of the group, whispering among themselves (a bit frightened lest the Master should overhear them): "Let's head Him off from this madness. He's already said that Lazarus' sickness is 'not unto death', so what's the use of asking for trouble and flying in the face of danger? Let's try to take cover! At any rate let's get Him to talk things over in committee. We may, at any rate, get the matter adjourned until the feeling against Him has died down a bit." But Thomas cuts in bluntly, a bit scornfully perhaps, and shames them all. "Let's go and die with Him!" And for sheer shame they had to fall in, because they knew he always said what he meant, and that he meant to go. "Doubting Thomas" saved the entire group from dishonour! Or consider the occasion when the Master is telling about His return Home: "Whither I go ye know, and the way ye know." Thomas responded (and as, I believe, for himself): "Master if You're going, how can we know the way, for we want to go where You go!" This was no admission of doubt—as though the way were unknowable. It is the anxious query born of a love that dreads separation! "We want to go with You; tell us, how can we know the way?" Until we see that this dull, silent, rather morose and untalkative man is really the greatest lover of the Master among them all.

Then followed the Cross and the general stampede of the group in the interests of their own skins. When they managed to reassemble, making their several ways to the Upper Room by roundabout routes, to avoid detection, "Thomas was not with them" when in the evening the Risen Master joined them. All kinds of speculation have been put forward to account for his absence, an absence for which he paid dearly (as do most people when they forsake Christian fellowship on any pretext!). For Thomas lost a full eight days' assurance of the Resurrection, and of joy and wonder and confidence and the inspiration of shared experience. And lost it all irrecoverably!

I venture to put forth another suggestion in addition to those commonly advanced (e.g. that he had never believed anything could happen once the Master was dead! That he concluded the Cause died when He died, and that, for himself, he'd better get back to work and nurse his disappointment—which, after all, had not been altogether unexpected! Or that he was covered with confusion at having done what the rest of the group had done—deserted the Master, that he was as sick with himself as he was with them, and didn't feel like having more to do with them, or facing the mutual recriminations which he knew were certain to be freely bandied about once they found themselves together again). My suggestion is—knowing already the kind of man he was—that Thomas was overcome with grief, and just couldn't face meeting anybody! That his heart was broken at the loss of Him he loved far better than life! That he could only nurse his wound in secret, and that he got clear away from everybody, perhaps into some quiet country place where he had once been with the Master; and that there, through his scalding tears, he faced the wreckage of his life and hopes and the empty loneliness of his heart, which he knew must become acuter, until death mercifully released him from its ache and throb. When a man like Thomas, a man of his reserved, slow, shrinking nature, loves, he loves! My own view is that Thomas was not there because he was away off getting a grip on himself, for he was all broken-up at the mere thought of living out his life without the Master.

When, after a terrible week—one of those weeks which seem like a century—he joins the group (remembering that his friends must be suffering as he was, and that he had a duty toward them) he is startled by their overflowing joy and their confident testimony: "We have seen the Lord!" They were full of their experience—could talk of nothing else, and were all on the tip-toe of expectation, for they might see Him again! Then Thomas' nature asserted itself. If this thing be true, it must be true beyond all doubt. Life would be insupportable if the Master were alive and he were not able to get close enough to Him—just once— to prove for all time (come what may in the future) that He is to be depended on, that He is the same as He had been in the dear, dead days beyond recall! That's the inwardness of Thomas' doubting. "Except I shall see", and it was not speculative, nor conceited, nor flippant, nor cynical, as the so-called doubt of some people is. Thomas' was not the doubt that is fed on argument and talk, nor was it the doubt of the agnostic who rather feels that the very title gives him a sort of distinction as a superior person. It was not the doubt which is just the expression of empty pride and an empty head, or that doesn't want to be disproved, and doesn't intend to be convinced. His was the doubt of soul travail—a very agony of "love" at its wits' end! It hadn't a sneer in its composition. He wanted to believe, more than he wanted anything in life. Only he must be sure! His doubt was just the voice of his temperament baptised by crushing sorrow—by that sort of sorrow that is positively poisonous. Thomas was a doubter, but he doubted because he loved so intensely— he was first a lover, a great lover of the Master. No shallow answer to a deep questioning could satisfy him. And he knew the Master well enough to be sure that He would understand, and would allow him to see and touch the nail-prints.

It is evident that the Master *did* understand, for when He came again to the group He didn't chide Thomas. No word of reproach or reproof passed His lips. He just let Thomas know how thoroughly and entirely He entered into His perplexity. How completely He knew him, and knew that in what he had said he was just being himself. And then He invited him to test His reality. Is it likely that the Master should be unaware of the longing that lay behind Thomas' slowness? Or that He should undervalue it? Believe me, some people's so-called perplexity means infinitely more to Him than some people's so-called certainty! The perplexity that presses on is far more like true religion than the certainty that stands still. The perplexity that seeks verification has a religious value far away beyond that of the certainty that engenders self-satisfaction. The perplexity that is dynamically sincere is out and away better than the certainty and cocksureness that is supinely orthodox. For the one is a pathway; the other just a paralysis. Thomas did reach out his hands, but not to touch the Master; only to cover his shamed face! One look into the Master's face, one word from Him is enough! Love, adoration, confidence, everything expressed itself: "My Lord: My God."

Mark you, a man like Thomas will never be a glib, religious phraseologist. It's not desirable that he should and certainly not Christ's desire! He'll never use great words, as some do, as counters of orthodoxy. No cheap and hollow "Hallelujahs" will come from him. Whatever he says has tremendous meaning for him. He's prepared to stand by its uttermost implication. From that hour he knew! Knowledge crowned love with courageous confidence: "With great power the disciples gave witness to the Resurrection of the Lord Jesus." And Thomas was among the foremost. His declaration of belief was actually a dedication of life. From then on he walked in the Way he had once been perplexed over. He knows now that it's not

Creed nor Form nor Ritual Word,
But simply following Thee!

Tradition takes him eastward to Persia, India and China. In India, the Syrian churches in Malabar are said to have been founded by him. It is believed also that he sought out the Wise Men and baptised them in the Christian Faith! Be that as it may, Thomas justified the Master's confidence, and only the Day will declare the great issues of his utter sincerity and its inexhaustible reward in the relationship with the Risen Lord which from that day he enjoyed.

Have I been talking about Thomas and those days of long ago? Rather has the Master Himself been talking to us all and calling us out to be His men. For He's alive, and He's the same yesterday, today and for ever!

How can we know the way? By beginning to tread it! And it will shine before you, more and more, to the Perfect Day.

XIII

JAMES, THE LORD'S BROTHER

THE identity of the various James's who attained to some measure of distinction in the early days of the Christian movement has always been one of the problems of New Testament students. Had it not been for a casual remark of Paul's, this one might have been lost to us in the general confusion that surrounds them. But he singles him out for special mention and identification; and so sets him forth as a significant example, for our following of him as he followed Christ, a supplementary inspiration to Christian faith.

Paul, like every true minister, authenticated his evangel by his experience. To this group of Gentile converts he recounts his own spiritual history—a story that never loses its charm to the reciter or the hearers—in order to remove any doubt from their minds regarding his authority as an Apostle, which false and self-seeking teachers were trying to subvert. So he tells how, after his conversion and his subsequent retreat in Arabia, he spent a fortnight in Jerusalem visiting Peter.

What a fortnight that must have been! It is not difficult to imagine Peter showing his guest—whose eagerness could easily tire out a fisherman far more accustomed to walking the cool damp planking of a boat than the hot pavements of the city—round the places which had become sacred from their association with Jesus, until the Temple Courts, and the way out to Bethany, and Solomon's Porch and its sheep-pool, and the Upper Room, and the Garden, and the very place on the hillside road where He had wept over

the city, and the Pavement in front of Pilate's Palace—
called in the Hebrew "Gabbatha", and the place called
"Calvary"—yes, that place most of all—were as familiar
to Paul as to Peter himself. Is it difficult to imagine
the thousand and one questions Paul put—all about Him.
Such a chance might never come again to the man whose
passion was to "know Him", and he took full advantage
of it.

For some reason he didn't meet any of the other Apostles
—perhaps because he was so busy picking the bones of
Peter's memory, preventing the night-watches that, together, they might be occupied with the Word. Peter had
so much to tell and Paul so much to learn, that even meal-
times were forgotten by these two men who esteemed the
words that He had spoken "more than their necessary
food". While as for other people—it was as though they
didn't exist to those two whose hearts burned within them
as they spoke of Him whom each had come to know in his
own way. One of them had persecuted Him. The other
had denied Him. But for both of them Calvary had covered
it all. Both had been forgiven, and both loved Him now
better than life itself. The bond between them was the
closest tie this earth knows. And, strangely, so strangely
that probably each forbore to speak of it to the other, each
of them felt that He was actually with them as they talked
of Him; that He was an invisible third in their company
of two. As indeed He was.

So the hours sped, and the fortnight passed, all too
quickly, and Paul had met none of the other Apostles except
one. And he was quite content to shoulder his pack (a few
books and parchments and an extra garment or two) and
get back to his job without repairing the omission. For
had He not met the Lord Himself, and spent the most
wonderful vacation of his life with one who had been an
actual eyewitness of His majesty? And was he not going
back as the bees go back from their excursions over the

clover fields and rose gardens and heather hills, just laden
with knowledge "sweeter than honey and the honeycomb"?
But the one other man he did meet was the one he would
have desired above all others to meet—James, the Lord's
brother. What passed between them we don't know—
except that we may be sure they each added fuel to
the fire in the other's heart. Paul learned some things
he dearly wanted to know about the Lord. And the Lord's
brother learned some things, from one who knew Him
only in spiritual communion, that even the closest earthly
kinship had never taught him. Paul saw the Lord in
James, not in facial resemblance or family likeness—that
counted for nothing—but in one who had become like
Him in character, and mind, and bearing and spirit by
association.

Paul never forgot his meeting with James. It is easier
to die than to forget some experiences. And there are some
people who, in one chance meeting, do more for us, make
a more indelible mark and a more imperishable impression
upon our minds and indeed ultimately upon our characters,
than all the sermons and books of a lifetime. Although
they may never know it (and they are of the order who
would never believe it) they are our everlasting benefactors
—and one day we shall have the opportunity of telling
them (thus making Heaven two Heavens for them, and
sending them hurrying off to the Saviour to lay yet another
trophy and tribute at His feet), I'm glad I ever met you!
It's something for us all to live for, that we may be that
sort of person and exhale that sort of undying influence—
of simple humanness touched to great issues by our actual
fellowship with Christ—and give to others some saving
gleams of His glory, the glory of life well lived.

James, the Lord's brother, was that kind of a man to
Paul. His meeting with him was one of the things that
made the Apostle what he became. Indeed, Paul never
attained to so high a flight, never aimed more truly at the

very heart of things than when he reproduced some of the things he learned on that visit to Jerusalem, some of the ethical indispensables he learnt from him who had learnt them from his brother, who had become his Lord. (It is, by the way, a fruitful study for Bible students to trace the influence of James, the Lord's brother, on the thought and theology of Paul.) That, however, is not our present purpose, which is, rather, to look at this man and see how, at first (and for a long time, indeed), he failed to realise his unique privilege and squandered days and powers he would afterwards have given his right eye to recall; how he did actually recover himself and turned his failure to good account, and became a man to figure in the lives of others. That is, he became what the New Testament understands by a "Christian".

He was the half-brother of Jesus, younger than He, His companion in the life of the village home, and all that that meant. They played together, went to the town school together, the elder brother keeping a watchful eye over the younger, protecting him from the school bullies, giving him hints about what to do and what not to do, helping him with his lessons, being, in fact, the "big brother" to him until such time as he no longer needed His protection and became himself, in turn, the "big brother" to the one below him—Joses. They were brought up together in the Synagogue, learning their Psalms and Sacred History and Commandments together. Together they wondered at the mysteries and glories of the springtime; passed through their baptism of sorrow together when Joseph died; and not improbably they occasionally clashed when it came to working together at the bench—for there is every chance for two people to get on each other's nerves when they're compelled to work together at monotonous routine in a narrow sphere, especially relatives, with their privilege of unrestrained speech!

Of course, James respected and admired his brother—

even though he evidently didn't understand Him. The hero-worship of a boy for his elder brother, who has been his pilot in the perplexing seas of the early years and of adolescence, never completely fades out. There can be little doubt, too, that the craftmanship of Jesus was of a high order, that He handled tools with a skill that told of careful and steady practice, that He turned out ploughs and yokes and door-beams of a quality that compelled admiration, especially from His own apprentice, which James very likely was. And, of course, He wouldn't put up with scamped work. The smallest commission had to be carried out with the most scrupulous attention to the standards of sound workmanship in that shop. Excuses weren't accepted as reasons, however confidently they might be put forward, when His eye fell on a bit of carpentering which didn't come up to the standard of that firm. And James knew it too.

Indeed, that was one of the things he couldn't understand about his brother, why He should be so particular about things that didn't seem to matter much. Another thing was His apparent indifference to making money when He had a clear chance. The "tricks of the trade" which every other tradesman in Nazareth resorted to were never allowed to be practised in His workshop. And then poor people, whose circumstances were well-known, were never pressed for their accounts. He insisted on their being treated with consideration. And if James ever asked or grumbled about such lost opportunities or such unusual leniencies he would be mystified by his brother's reference to "My Father's business". That term evidently set a standard for Him which James simply couldn't understand and, with a Jew's flair for the right side of a bargain, certainly didn't appreciate.

But there, his brother was different—there was no denying it. And though he might ridicule Him sometimes, especially when He declined to do something that everyone else would have done, or when He was determined on some course being taken that, from a business point of view, led nowhere, he always respected His character. In his inmost mind he knew that He was pure gold, and he was secretly proud of it. If only He hadn't been so unconventionally religious. Not that He was ever slack—or permitted slackness in the household about family prayer or attendance at the Synagogue and its services and feasts and festivals. But He had a disconcerting way of connecting God with things that really had nothing to do with religion—at any rate, no other folk did it. And He most evidently preferred to say His prayers in the fields; and sometimes He would be out all night on the hills, and come back to the shop next day strangely uplifted, not wanting any food, but quietly speaking about the "bread of God". No! James couldn't understand his brother, and if anyone had told him (what was afterward written about those very days) that "He was full of wisdom and the grace of God was upon Him", he'd have been more mystified than ever.

Then one day there came to Nazareth rumours about a strange man who was preaching down South on the banks of the Jordan, and baptising people who publicly confessed their sins. All kinds of hidden things were being owned up to, and all sorts of people were being drawn into this weird kind of Revival. Until at last a few of the lake fishermen said they were going off to see for themselves, and they didn't come back. Then, one day, James' brother handed over the shop to him and declared that He, too, was going down to Bethabara. One can almost hear James saying: "Of course, *you* would go. This is what we've all been expecting." But his cynical comment evoked no reply. Just a quiet farewell, and a handing over of the business, and his brother was gone. By and by disquieting stories about what had happened down there began to filter back to Nazareth. And while He was still the subject of village gossip, James' brother returned, probably timing His return just on the eve of the Sabbath. And what a Sabbath that was! The Synagogue service ending in an uproar, and a mob, and a determined effort to get rid for ever of the blasphemous carpenter who had dared to identify Himself, in a public declaration, with the subject of the Sacred Scriptures.

It put an affront upon His family (of which James had now become the head), which was a sore trial to them. When the day's work was done and the shop closed and the lamp lighted behind closed doors, they argued pro and con His sanity. And though His mother had some things hidden in her heart which would have shed light on their perplexity, she kept them to herself. So, next day, James gave out to the village that his brother had a devil and was mad, and that they wanted it to be known that none of the family believed in His claims.

Once or twice during the next three years, when the name of Jesus was on every tongue and it was common knowledge that the authorities were only watching their opportunity to take Him on some serious charge and put Him to death, James did try to dissuade His brother, in the name of the family, to give up His strange ways and come back home and live down His reputation for queerness, and at least spare them all the ignominy of having an executed criminal in their family record. With what success we know!

It is almost inconceivable that James, at least, could be so callous when it came to the point, as to leave Him to bear, without any support, the multiplied agonies and humiliations of the last few days. But he did. He even left his mother (who by that time had evidently repented of her earlier compliance with James' attitude of "save the family name and business" by disavowing any sympathy with Jesus and His outlandish ways; and indeed had, it would almost seem, come to an open breach with him about it) to suffer, unsupported, the tortures of the Crucifixion day. But his unbelief was obstinate, though always, behind it, lay a deep respect for what he knew his brother (apart from His religious aberrations) to be—a Man the like of whom he had never looked on or was ever likely to look on.

Why have I tried to recreate the circumstances and sketch the character of James, the Lord's brother?

Only that the contrast between what he was and what he became, between what he squandered and what he recovered, between the anti-Christ influence he wielded and the pro-Christian influence he acquired, may magnify the grace and power of his Lord and ours, and encourage us to the full consciousness of our relationship and privilege, and to the full exercise of our life's most precious opportunities.

For this was the man who became the President of the Council in the earliest organisation of the Christian Church; with the authority not of the position (for the difference between a New Testament bishopric and that which the term connotes today is the difference between exact opposites) but of one who could interpret to his colleagues the mind of their Master in the spirit of their Master. This was the man who helped to engrave the name of Jesus more deeply on the heart of Paul ; the man who, subsequently, more searchingly and convincingly than any other, from his own intimate knowledge of his brother who had become his Lord, set down in the form of a treatise on Christian living, in terms which everyone could understand (only too well!), the inescapable obligations of every Christian man.

For it is James, the Lord's brother, who insists upon the Christianising of every personal relationship and social attachment as the real work of faith, and labour of love, and patience of hope of the believer in his brother. He knew *what* his brother was. Better still, and vastly more important, he had come to know *who* his brother was. And that's what brought about the change in him.

After the Resurrection, and the slight stir (and it was but a slight stir) which the execution of Jesus and the subsequent events made, had just about died down, He suddenly appeared to James. No details of that momentous interview are given. Just the bare fact that "He was seen of James". I like to think it was in the workshop, as he was busy on a job for one of the villagers, with the sweet smell of wood shavings and sawdust in the air, and the tools scattered round in the orderly confusion the good workman delights in, that James was arrested by hearing his name called in the old, familiar way. And that, looking up, he saw his brother, and recognised Him as his Lord. And that there and then the confession was made, the vows were registered, and promises spoken, and the assurance given that changed life for ever for James, and wrote another name in the Lamb's Book of Life, among them that follow the Lamb whithersoever He goeth.

What does it all mean to us? Just this—that the circumstances of our lives are as uniquely favourable to our knowledge of the Lord as were James'. Life has no higher possibility than this—which every life has, that we may each know Him, in relation to our own nature and our affairs and our secret history, as no one else can know Him. But with this difference—we begin more advantaged than James was. He came to know the Risen Lord only after all those barren years. We have known none other than the Living Christ if we have known Him at all. Any excuse he might have advanced it is not open to us to offer. Hence the warning he would certainly cry out upon us—not to lose the glory that lies in the familiar, not to lose ourselves as he nearly lost himself, by sheer indifference until it was almost too late—has an urgent edge upon it which we had better not try to evade. For our danger is as much greater than his as is our privilege.

"James, the Lord's brother"—what a title by which to

be known! Listen: "Whoso doeth the Will of God, the same is My brother."

And there are potential Pauls whom you are daily meeting. Blessed is that man of whom, in days to come, one of them will say, erecting thereby his own spiritual landmark: "I saw the Lord's brother."

XIV

ZEBEDEE

An Ordinary Man—and Christ

ONE OF the characteristic features of the Bible which increasingly endears it to those whose endeavour it is to make it the guide and rule of life, is its frank humanity. It is essentially a record of human life in its reactions to the Divine care and will and promises. It tells the story of "life", divine and eternal, in terms of life, human and temporal. It not only declares principles and precepts but demonstrates them in personalities. And herein is seen the Wisdom of God, for while few can fully comprehend Truth in abstract expression, all can take in the lessons set forth in lives of men and women in their personal, wilful attitudes toward its demands, at any rate sufficiently so to profit alternatively by their encouragement or warning.

That is why we come again and again to the Bible and find something fresh and stimulating, either to penitence or persistence, in its straightforward and obviously sincere chronicles of lives like our own. For experience of life gives us penetrating insights into the qualities and vagaries of our own nature, and so we bring an increasingly reliable discrimination of the vital things to these records, which thus become actually contemporary.

Nor is this value limited to the outstanding Bible characters. It goes without saying that from the lives of Moses, David, Paul and many another there come to us lessons and assurances of value beyond telling. But equally important in their significance to ourselves are the accounts given (most frequently brief, mere allusions rather than actual records) of much obscurer men—men who filled only a small part in the moving life of their day; not planets but fixed stars of but minor magnitude in the firmament of faith. Equally important because, in the main, their capacities and opportunities are within our own reach.

It is the way of the Bible to take some quite obscure man and, without advancing him to any prominence, to make the story of his relationship to God stand out with vividly arresting power. And this particularly in respect of his contact with Christ.

Every man who came into any sort of touch with Him achieved thereby a kind of immortality, even the people who knew Him as the "Carpenter"; the women who brought their babies; the thieves who were crucified with Him. And the very fact of the obscurity of the many who, in this way, stand for a moment in Light and then are hidden in silence carries its message.

In the main they form a company of anonymous, ordinary, commonplace people, who bear witness to the possibility of glorifying God on the usual levels of undistinguished life. Or, alternatively, they bear witness to the danger of the usual occupations and preoccupations of life blinding men to Truth, and binding them to their engrossments to their undoing.

They are neither prominent people nor yet entirely negligible; neither very bad nor very good; neither very brilliant nor very stupid—just ordinary. And the fact that there are so many of them in what may be termed the "dramatis personae" of the New Testament declares in altogether unmistakable fashion that the Christian religion is not a thing apart from life, as most people have to live it.

The more we know of Christ and His way of life, the more convinced we are that there's nothing unpractical, highfalutin, artificial—nothing that needs some specially

favourable setting—about it. In order to bring this home
(with all that it means to have any Truth brought home),
and knowing full well that it will mean the raising of
inescapable issues, let us look at one such ordinary man—
and Christ.

Zebedee was the father of James and John, and in com-
parison with them seems to be much less worthy of consideration. He was a fisherman and that he had some
success in his calling is evident by the "hired servants".
He remained a fisherman after Christ had invaded the
family circle, called his sons to discipleship, and drawn his
wife into the group of women who followed Him up and
down the land "ministering".

Sometimes Zebedee is held up to criticism and reprobation
because he did not leave all when his sons did—a warning
example of those who put business and home, fishing boats,
and nets and market prices and the "pull" of the world's
life, before Christ. Sometimes he is instanced as a terrible
case of a man who had become too old, deaf, and hardened
in sin, too set in his own wilful ways, to heed Christ. He
is pointed out as one whose emotions, fluid and warm
enough in youth, had crystallised into hard unchangeable
attitudes; referred to as one who was overborne in any
intentions he might have had by the conservatism which
is always to the fore in successful men of business, and
made thereby unwilling and indisposed—even unable—to
take a risk. Stress is laid on the fact that on another occasion
it was his wife who brought James and John prominently
before Christ, seeking special honour for them in His Kingdom. As a matter of fact his absence from that scene does
him credit, seeing what *was* the motive which prompted
the audacious request! If he was ever consulted about it
—which is much to be doubted—his absence is just an
evidence of fine feeling and of his fuller knowledge and
truer perceptions of Christ.

Now look closer at the narrative. It is evident that all

such strictures upon Zebedee are undeserved and purely gratuitous; that these are not the lessons of his life at all.

Zebedee obviously made no remonstrance at the sudden calling of James and John. Such would certainly have been found a place in the Gospels if only to put on record their wholehearted response to Christ. Does not the fact that he uttered no word to deter them, though it must have meant a good deal to his business and plans for the future, point to his own otherwise unrecorded belief in Christ? Does it not rather suggest that he may himself have been a disciple of John the Baptist, and had taught his sons to recognise Christ? Had there perhaps been a secret interview with the Master, and earnest talk about the Kingdom? "How can I best serve You?" Zebedee might have asked. "Let Me have your sons," had come the searching reply, until Christ and Zebedee entirely understood each other and trusted each other.

There is more than a hint that he had none too easy a time with his wife! Quite obviously she was an ambitious, pushful, voluble woman—a "climber". She managed her sons, and it's certain she wasn't averse from trying to manage Zebedee too. I shouldn't wonder if she objected strongly to the sons "going off like that"—until she heard there was a Kingdom and crowns in it. Then she went herself! Perhaps her over-forwardness made Zebedee even more shrinking, his faith all the more sincere.

Is it too much to suggest that when James and John went he supported them by prayer and gift? They were clearly the affluent members of the Twelve (recall John's adoption of Mary into his own home), and the money came from Zebedee. It cost him something to lose their labour, but he wasn't content to let that alone count as his contribution. He saw to it that they, and the Master, didn't lack.

Zebedee is set forth for the encouragement of the ordinary man, whose grateful recognition of Christ does not mean that he has to leave his business and start preaching, but just that he has got to be Salt in the community and Light in the world. He is a type of the honest, undistinguished, substantial men of whom Christ's Kingdom is advanced by their quality in home and business circles; the men who sense God in business or professional life and through it. Too old, it may be, for engagements in public and organised forms of Christian service; a bit too set in their ways to follow the younger crowd; committed to economic responsibilities affecting the well-being of others; but never unsympathetic, uninterested, unfaithful and never even thinking of life as having any more supreme relationship than its relationship to Christ and His cause.

Such an one has much the harder part. Far easier is it to go and preach than to stay and translate faith into convincing conduct. For here is no applause and not even recognition; just the support of conscience, and the recompense of communion. The foes to be met in the world of affairs, in competition that is not always fair, in an atmosphere often deadening, in relative isolation—are far more insistent and challenging than those which James and John have to overcome.

For Zebedee there is just the humdrum work of fishing and selling, and net-mending, and fishing again. Many are the tests of temper—storms, flat calms, and the sheer perverseness of others. Doubtless there were many occasions when consistent Christian character had to rebuke the too free conversation round the boats and in the market. In that "climate" Zebedee develops character as fine as any achieved by the ministry, in many respects finer.

But it is of Zebedee and his like that the Kingdom is being steadily advanced. Christ has, in them, points of contact with the world, radiating centres of influence reaching to those who never hear James and John. He may not be an Apostle (in their sense), but he is a "living Epistle", known and read of all men. And in the final reckoning there will probably be no more honour for the sons who went than for father who let them go, and took the work to his heart, and gave to its support, and exemplified what they proclaimed.

Do you sometimes become discouraged because your Christian life is so ordinary? Are you tempted to belittle the value of your witness because you are but a voice in the chorus and not a soloist? And tempted to give up idealism and stick to "fish", just because there's no thrill in the steady, uneventful, apparently unproductive disciple-ship to which you are bound? Take fresh heart from this story of Zebedee. Christ wants you where He has found and keeps you. "Abide in your calling" with Him, and keep your interest in the movement of His Kingdom alive by determined witness, informed prayer, and by giving that costs something.

For the story and its meaning amount to this—that Zebedee can live the Christian life in a fishing boat, large or small, and its modern equivalent of office, factory, school, home, hospital, and can there be not only a bread-winner but a soul-winner if he will. For Christ lives in Him.

> I'm just a cog in life's vast wheel,
> That daily makes the same old trip.
> But what a joy it is to feel
> That but for me the wheel might slip!
> 'Tis something, after all, to jog
> Along and be a first-class cog.

XV

"ART THOU ONE OF THIS MAN'S DISCIPLES?"

John xviii. 25

THE SCENE that day in the palace of the High Priest was in every respect a miniature of the scene in this our own day. There, in the centre of two irreconcilable groups, was Jesus Christ. By far the larger of these groups (the other, indeed, was a mere handful) was made up of people coldly and contemptuously indifferent to Him, or wildly hostile and loudly insistent upon His death by the ignominious and cruel method of crucifixion. There were sinister influences at work stimulating their frenzy, of which probably most of them were completely unaware. This sophisticated age of ours is not the first in which the art of exploiting the herd instinct had been successfully practised; and that group, aroused to passionate, thoughtless determination, meant just one thing, and shouted it: "We will not have this Man."

The other group was hardly a group at all, consisting of under one dozen men and a few women. Too frightened even to keep together, they hovered around the edge of the shouting rabble, some of them silently praying—the while condemning themselves for their lack of courage in not standing by Him. All of them were hoping, yet fearing the worst. They knew Him, and in their own poor way loved Him. They were stunned and dazed at what had recently happened, although they had been aware for some time that trouble was brewing, for He never attempted to hide it from them—and He knew. When the blow of His arrest and now of His arraignment before this mockery of a tribunal fell upon them, it was devastating. They scattered and sheltered from their own danger behind the agitation of the crowd, silent and cowed and heart-sick, fearful lest they should be discovered and themselves be haled before the cynical young Roman judge, for in such an atmosphere anything might happen.

Quiet, unmoved, unafraid stands Jesus Christ, fully aware of everything going on in both groups, and of what it would immediately lead to. No harsh thoughts of blame invade His peace; no words of remonstrance escape His lips. In His heart there is only forgiveness for His enemies and concern for His disorganised friends. The stage is set for the Great Drama! And the setting has not been altered down all the years. The dramatis personæ are just the same today: Jesus Christ; His disciples; the world.

To one of that scattered handful of men who had ventured nearer to the fire round which the larger group had gathered, some of the agitators, thinking they recognised him, said rudely, possibly threateningly: "Art thou one of this Man's disciples?" It may be they thought that if he were a disciple he should not be skulking away from Jesus and possible danger. They may have had a sneer and contempt in their query, for no one admires a coward. Not unlikely there may have been a thinly disguised menace in it, or was it just mocking derision? At any rate, whatever it was, the man they accosted gave them a poor sort of impression of the influence Jesus had had upon him. It is quite certain that he made no converts by what he revealed to them of Christ's power and inspiration. They had not thought much of Him before; they thought even less now that they had met one of His followers at close quarters. Oh, the tragedy of it! That He should have been betrayed in the very hour of His love's unutterable sacrifice; that He should be wounded in the house of His friends.

Do you see how modern it all is? Jesus Christ; ourselves; the world—and the world taking its measure of Him, coming to its conclusions about Him and strengthening and justifying its indifference to His claims and its unbelief in His promises by its open discoveries of us. For let us be in no doubt about this—we stand between Christ and the world. Our lives are either a transparent medium through which He is clearly seen—"magnified" is the term Paul used—or they distort and obscure Him. His influence upon us is a thing discernible and self-declaratory. There is no mistaking a life which is steadily responding to His control. We are either making faith in Him easier or harder for the people in our world; we furnish them either with incentives or excuses. Which is it?

The story is often told of the discovery of the planet Neptune by Mr. Adam, the astronomer. He was set on the track of some great and powerful star-world, much too far away to be seen through the then furthest penetrating telescope, by its clearly evident influence upon the already charted course of another planet, Uranus! He noticed that whenever Uranus came into a certain place in the heavens, in its regular orbit, it was obviously deflected in a certain direction by coming under the powerful attractive influence of some invisible planet. That hidden influence and the response to it were so constant that only one explanation of the phenomenon could be deduced—the presence of that great Neptune, which is now known to be the centre of a planetory system all its own. Which incident is a parable. Does the quality of your life suggest to your world that you are under a Secret Influence and Control for which no explanation but One is tenable? Is it likely that anybody knowing you, as well as people do know one another today, will ever be set off on their own track in search and discovery of Him whose Name you bear? Is it likely they would ever turn to you, with confidence that you could aid their quest, and say: "Sir, we would see *your* Jesus"?

Does it ever happen? Nothing is surer in contemporary life than that. The half-surprised, half-sarcastic interrogation which challenged Peter that day is repeated to us, or perhaps more often *about* us, whenever the world learns of our Christian profession and comes up against our quality.

Let me attempt to paraphrase the world's present-day expression of this soul-searching query.

"*Art thou one of this man's disciples?* But you're not very like Him, are you? He did carry His ideas about God into all His daily life, didn't He? Not that we *always* agree with His ideas. But you *do* agree with Him about them, don't you, and they don't enter into *your daily life* much, do they?"

"*Art thou one of this man's disciples?* But surely He loved people and did things for them, and never tried to get anything out of them for Himself: and you're not like that, are you? We never think of *you* as anything but quite characteristically self-assertive, and *you* don't love people much, do you? Why, only yesterday, we heard you ourselves saying some very cutting things about someone who had displeased you, and it was about another disciple too, was it not? And didn't He say that His disciples were people who would always be recognisable by the fact that they loved one another?"

"*Art thou one of this man's disciples?* But surely He said that His disciples were to put the interests of the Kingdom of God first, before every other thing in life? That they were to seek its extension as of supreme importance, supreme over every other interest? He did it, too, as well as talked about it: we know that. But you don't, do you? He gave everything He had, even his life, for what He called the Kingdom of God, didn't He? But *you* don't give much, do you? Or do you do it anonymously? It's hardly like you, if you do! As a matter of fact, you are really quite keen on getting things for yourself, money

and praise and honour and the good things of life—everyone knows that, now—aren't you?"

"*Art thou one of this man's disciples?* But surely He said
that He didn't do His own will; that it was God's will
that He did! And you have always been determined—
quite determined—to do what you like, haven't you? And
to make others do what you like, too, if you can. That's
why you have lost your children and made your home so
unhappy, isn't it? And that's why you are unhappy yourself, isn't it? Just as unhappy as we try to forget we
are."

"*Art thou one of this man's disciples?* Then how can you
be so narrowminded, and so critical and censorious of those
who do not happen to agree with you? He wasn't, was
He? Why, it is His broadminded sympathy and appreciation of others (even when they were not actually on His
side) that causes us to admire Him so. Did not somebody
once say about Him that 'He knew what was in men'?
That He went to the trouble of finding out the other man's
point of view? Wasn't that what made Him such a Friend
to all sorts of unlikely people? But you're not like that,
are you now?"

"*Art thou one of this man's disciples?* Then *why* do you
do and say so many mean things? And why are you so
lethargic and slack, and why so fussy about things which
cannot be of any great importance if what He taught is
true? And so undependable? And so ready to fall in with
our frankly pagan ways when it seems advantageous to you
to do so? Of course, you may as well know we don't
respect you for it; as a matter of fact we rather despise
you. For, certainly, we know it is not a bit like Him. Our
quarrel with you is not because you declare yourself Christian, but because you are not Christian enough! And there
are times when we wish, for His sake, and your own as
well, that you'd stop talking of yourself as a Christian and
stop using His Name so freely."

"Art thou one of this man's disciples? Then *why* are you warming yourself, when He's giving Himself? Why are you silent about Him when, by every token, we of the world are in such dire need of the things He certainly stands for and is supposed to be able to impart? Things like peace and good-will and independent joy and un-suspicion, mutual understanding and unanxious life and reverence and social justice and brotherly love! You don't seem to have learnt much from Him, do you? You are not suffering much to bring the spirit of His Gospel to bear upon our own disordered and frantic and hopelessly in-volved life, are you? Art thou one of this Man's disciples? It is hard to believe."

So the world might speak, more in pity than in anger. Often it does speak with a wistfulness in its tone rather than with the lash of a whip in its tongue. For the world knows full well that it needs Him. That fact has been hammered into its consciousness by a long succession of dreary failures and the total collapse of hopes built upon itself. It knows it can no more guide itself in the storm that is beating upon it than a ship-master can steer his vessel by its own masthead light. Make no mistake about it, the world knows its need of Him and would seek Him if only the way to Him was not blocked with slow-moving traffic; if only His avowed disciples were not between Christ and the world He has redeemed and alone can save.

If that is what the world says to us, what does *He* say to us in all this? Well, that entirely depends upon how we take the world's scathing comment. If we are resentful, and self-excusing and determined to pay no heed, and self-justifying and inwardly proud and stubborn, He says nothing. At any rate nothing that we can hear; our atti-tude of stubborn self-satisfaction puts us out of hearing distance of Him. Deaf ears make a dumb Christ. And all the while He is yearning to reach the world through us, and we are holding up His purpose, for He loves the world just as much as He loves His church. The sacred records of His love are set in terms of sacrificial self-giving on behalf of both alike. *But* if we are humbled and confused and ashamed and bitterly penitent; if we seek refuge from our self-condemnation in Him, in His wounds and His open arms; if we creep to Him as when we were boys and had lost a fight or failed in an examination we crept home with our wounds or our humbled pride to the dear shelter of understanding and love, He will speak and to some purpose! By His Word and by His creative Spirit He will do for each of us individually what He did for Peter, who was the first of a long line of would-be disciples to feel the stinging challenge of this question.

Trace the steps by which He leads out of the shadowland into the sunlight:

(1) He restores our self respect by putting Himself *to us* a question with a positively tremendous underlying assumption. He asks: "Lovest thou Me?" And He suggests by that very enquiry that, in spite of everything, it is still possible we may. That our capacity for responsive love may have become sadly impaired by the very lightness of our regard for His sacrificial love and the obligations it imposes upon us—but that it's not obliterated.

And on our stammering confession He

(2) Blots out the past completely—to be remembered no more for ever, cast into the Crimson Sea of eternal forgetfulness; driven, like the scapegoat of old time, into the desert-land of No Memory!

And

(3) Gives us the unencumbered opportunity of a new beginning. It has been said that the Christian life is

just this—"a succession of fresh starts". And how good for us that it is! That He accepts our discredited professions, and looks upon our avowals of love as being truer to our intentions than our denials of discipleship are, and *trusts us again* with a new commission to represent Him to the world.

And

(4) He assures us of the constant aid of His Spirit— His own life linked with ours and lived out in ours for the building up of a convincing moral personality, and the carrying out by the perfection of that personality of a ministry of cleansing, quickening, illuminating, guiding influence upon the world—the making of a full personal contribution to the establishment of His Kingdom and rule in the lives and affairs and relationships of men in their nearest and their furthermost reaches.

JESUS . . . OURSELVES . . . THE WORLD

"Art thou one of this Man's disciples?"

"Lovest thou Me?"

"Yea, Lord, though my face is shamed and I cannot see Thee for my tears, and my heart is broken—Thou knowest that I love Thee!"

"Arise: let us go hence—together."